28th International Conference on Computational Linguistics (COLING 2020)

Systems Demonstrations

Held online due to COVID-19

Barcelona, Spain
8 - 13 December 2020

ISBN: 978-1-7138-2523-4

COLING 2020

**The 27th International Conference
on Computational Linguistics**

Proceedings of System Demonstrations

December 8-13, 2020
Barcelona, Spain (Online)

Preface

This volume contains papers from the system demonstration session of the 28th International Conference on Computational Linguistics (COLING 2020) held in online. Due to the COVID-19 pandemic the conference is held fully online under the auspices of the International Committee on Computational Linguistics (ICCL).

The demonstration session complements the conference's presentation and poster sessions and is focused on working software systems that are the tangible outcomes of research on computational linguistics.

As a result of a rigorous review process, we accepted 16 papers out of 55 submissions. The program committee consisted of 88 members and two chairs from both academia and industry. Each member evaluated 1-2 papers, which amounted to at least two reviews per paper. The acceptance criteria we followed during the selection process included the quality of work as well as the utility and demonstrability potential of the presented systems. Consequently, most of the accepted systems are user-interactive and feature rich graphical user interfaces.

First and foremost we would like to thank the program committee for their hard work and dedication to help make this event a success. Our special thanks also go to the people who made COLING 2020 and this volume possible. We thank General Chair, Donia Scott (University of Sussex), Program Co-Chairs, Nuria Bel (Pompeu Fabra University) and Chengqing Zong (Chinese Academy of Sciences), Local Organization Co-Chairs, Leo Wanner (Pompeu Fabra University), Horacio Saggion (Pompeu Fabra University), Mónica Domínguez (Pompeu Fabra University), Publication Co-Chairs, Derek Wong (University of Macau), Liang Huang (Oregon State University), Yang Zhao (Chinese Academy of Sciences), Virtual Infrastructure Co-Chairs, Paul Piwek (The Open University), Lluís Padró Cirera (Polytechnic University of Catalonia), Luis Espinosa Anke (Cardiff University), Publicity Co-Chairs, Ghazaleh Kazeminejad (University of Colorado Boulder), Tiejun Zhao (Harbin Institute of Technology), Ted Pedersen (University of Minnesota), Anna Rogers (University of Copenhagen), Sponsorship Co-Chairs, Feiyu Xu (SAP), Alexander Löser (Beuth University of Applied Sciences Berlin), Jose Manuel Gómez Pérez (Expert System Iberia), Virtual Social Chair, Esther Seyffarth (Heinrich Heine University), Web Co-Chairs, Laura Pérez-Mayos (Pompeu Fabra University), Amita Misra (IBM Watson), Ethics Advisory Group, Tim Baldwin (University of Melbourne), Amanda Stent (Bloomberg LP), Emily Bender (University of Washington), Dirk Hovy (Bocconi University), Ted Pedersen (University of Minnesota), Pascale Fung (Hong Kong University of Science and Technology), Saif M. Mohammad (National Research Council Canada), and our Local Support, Joana Clotet (Pompeu Fabra University) for their tireless work.

Michal PTASZYNSKI and Bartsz ZIOLKO
COLING 2020 Demonstration Program Co-Chairs
07 November 2020

Demonstration Co-Chairs:

Michal Ptaszynski, Kitami Institute of Technology
Bartosz Ziolko, Techmo

Program Committee:

Lars Ahrenberg, Linköping University
Eiji Aramaki, NAIST
Elizabeth Boschee, Information Sciences Institute
Yi Cai, South China University of Technology
Vittorio Castelli, IBM Research AI
Angel Chang, Simon Fraser University
Nancy Chen, Institute for Infocomm Research, A*STAR
Zhumin Chen, Shandong University
Li Cheng, Xinjiang Technical Institute of Physics & Chemistry, Chinese Academy of Sciences
Christian Chiarcos, Goethe-Universität Frankfurt am Main
Christos Christodoulopoulos, Amazon Research
Danilo Croce, University of Roma, Tor Vergata
Patrick Ehlen, Loop AI Labs
Michael Elhadad, Ben Gurion University
Andrea Esuli, ISTI-CNR
Yang Feng, Institute of Computing Technology, Chinese Academy of Sciences
Chong Feng, Beijing Institute of Technology
Radu Florian, IBM Research
Dimitris Galanis, Institute for Language and Speech Processing, Athena Research Center
Michael Gamon, Microsoft Research
Siva Reddy Gangireddy, Voysis
Roxana Girju, University of Illinois, Urbana-Champaign
Xianpei Han, Institute of Software, Chinese Academy of Sciences
Tianyong Hao, School of Computer Science, South China Normal University
Kenji Hatano, Doshisha University
Yifan He, Alibaba Group
Ales Horak, Masaryk University
Magdalena Igras-Cybulska, AGH University of Science and Technology
Shajith Ikbal, IBM Research AI, India.
Iustina Ilisei, Cognizant Technology Solutions
Adam Jatowt, Kyoto University
Wenbin Jiang, Baidu Inc.
Mamoru Komachi, Tokyo Metropolitan University
Valia Kordoni, Humboldt-Universität zu Berlin
Marek Kubis, Adam Mickiewicz University
Carolin Lawrence, NEC Laboratories Europe
John Lee, City University of Hong Kong
Yves Lepage, Waseda University
Nikola Ljubešić, Jožef Stefan Institute
Wolfgang Maier, Mercedes-Benz AG
Benjamin Marie, NICT

Stella Markantonatou, ILSP/R.C. "Athena"
Kazuya Mera, Hiroshima City University
Makoto Miwa, Toyota Technological Institute
Taesun Moon, IBM Research
Mikolaj Morzy, Poznan University of Technology
Philippe Muller, IRIT, University of Toulouse
Koji Murakami, Rakuten Institute of Technology NY
Preslav Nakov, Qatar Computing Research Institute, HBKU
Vincent Ng, University of Texas at Dallas
Eric Nichols, Honda Research Institute Japan
Jagna Nieuwazny, Kitami Institute of Technology
Karol Nowakowski, Kitami Institute of Technology
Pierre Nugues, Lund University
Maciej Ogrodniczuk, Institute of Computer Science, Polish AcadeInstitute of Physicsmy of Sciences
Naoaki Okazaki, Tokyo Institute of Technology
Constantin Orasan, University of Surrey
Aasish Pappu, Spotify Research
Yannick Parmentier, University of Lorraine
Siddharth Patwardhan, Apple
Prokopis Prokopidis, ILSP/Athena RC
Guilin Qi, Southeast University
Likun Qiu, Minjiang University
Carlos Ramisch, Aix Marseille University, CNRS, LIS
German Rigau, UPV/EHU
Robert Ross, Technological University Dublin
Rafal Rzepka, Hokkaido University
Saurav Sahay, Intel Labs
Satoshi Sekine, Riken, AIP
Michel Simard, NRC
Vivek Srikumar, University of Utah
Mihai Surdeanu, University of Arizona
Kaveh Taghipour, Qritive
Christoph Teichmann, Bloomberg LP
Nadi Tomeh, LIPN, Université Sorbonne Paris Nord
Andrea Varga, CUBE
Yannick Versley, Amazon Alexa
Rui Wang, Alibaba Group
Aleksander Wawer, Institute of Computer Science, Polish Academy of Sciences
Guillaume Wisniewski, Université Paris and LLF
Kun Xu, Tencent AI Lab
Ruifeng Xu, Harbin Institute of Technology, Shenzhen
Tae Yano, Expedia Group
Motoki Yatsu, Aoyama Gakuin University
Dongdong Zhang, Microsoft Research Asia
Guangyou Zhou, School of Computer Science, Central China Normal University
Imed Zitouni, Google
Pierre Zweigenbaum, LIMSI, CNRS, Université Paris-Saclay

Table of Contents

December 9 (Wed), 2020, 16:00–16:30
Session 1 Tools for facilitating research and everyday use

MaintNet: A Collaborative Open-Source Library for Predictive Maintenance Language Resources
Farhad Akhbardeh, Travis Desell and Marcos Zampieri

DART: A Lightweight Quality-Suggestive Data-to-Text Annotation Tool
Ernie Chang, Jeriah Caplinger, Alex Marin, Xiaoyu Shen and Vera Demberg

Fast Word Predictor for On-Device Application
Huy Tien Nguyen, Khoi Tuan Nguyen, Anh Tuan Nguyen and Thanh Lac Thi Tran

XplaiNLI: Explainable Natural Language Inference through Visual Analytics
Aikaterini-Lida Kalouli, Rita Sevastjanova, Valeria de Paiva, Richard Crouch and Mennatallah El-Assady

An Online Readability Leveled Arabic Thesaurus
Zhengyang Jiang, Nizar Habash and Muhamed Al Khalil

TrainX – Named Entity Linking with Active Sampling and Bi-Encoders
Tom Oberhauser, Tim Bischoff, Karl Brendel, Maluna Menke, Tobias Klatt, Amy Siu, Felix Alexander
Gers and Alexander Löser

Annobot: Platform for Annotating and Creating Datasets through Conversation with a Chatbot
Rafał Poświata and Michał Perełkiewicz

Arabic Curriculum Analysis
Hamdy Mubarak, Shimaa Amer, Ahmed Abdelali and Kareem Darwish

Epistolary Education in 21st Century: A System to Support Composition of E-mails by Students to Superiors in Japanese
Kenji Ryu and Michal Ptaszynski

December 11 (Fri), 2020, 16:00–16:30
Session 2 Tools for NLP applications to other fields

Ve'rdd. Narrowing the Gap between Paper Dictionaries, Low-Resource NLP and Community Involvement
Khalid Alnajjar, Mika Hämäläinen, Jack Rueter and Niko Partanen

Demo Application for the AutoGOAL Framework
Suilan Estevez-Velarde, Alejandro Piad-Morffis, Yoan Gutiérrez, Andres Montoyo, Rafael Muñoz-Guillena
and Yudivián Almeida Cruz

Semantic search with domain-specific word-embedding and production monitoring in Fintech
Mojtaba Farmanbar, Nikki Van Ommeren and Boyang Zhao

CogniVal in Action: An Interface for Customizable Cognitive Word Embedding Evaluation
Nora Hollenstein, Adrian van der Lek and Ce Zhang

Ve′rdd. Narrowing the Gap between Paper Dictionaries, Low-Resource NLP and Community Involvement

Khalid Alnajjar   Mika Hämäläinen   Jack Rueter   Niko Partanen
Department of Digital Humanities
University of Helsinki and Rootroo Ltd
`firstname.lastname@helsinki.fi`

Abstract

We present an open-source online dictionary editing system, Ve′rdd, that offers a chance to re-evaluate and edit grassroots dictionaries that have been exposed to multiple amateur editors. The idea is to incorporate community activities into a state-of-the-art finite-state language description of a seriously endangered minority language, Skolt Sami. Problems involve getting the community to take part in things above the pencil-and-paper level. At times, it seems that the native speakers and the dictionary oriented are lacking technical understanding to utilize the infrastructures which might make their work more meaningful in the future, i.e. multiple reuse of all of their input. Therefore, our system integrates with the existing tools and infrastructures for Uralic language masking the technical complexities behind a user-friendly UI.

1   Introduction

We present an open-source dictionary editing tool[1] called Ve′rdd[2]. The tool has been and currently is under active development to cater for the needs of Skolt Sami (*ISO 639-2: sms*) speaking language community and their on-going project on modernizing a Finnish-Skolt Sami paper dictionary (see (Alnajjar et al., 2020)). Although Skolt Sami is severely endangered with its 300 native speakers (Moseley, 2010), a great deal of NLP tools have been developed for it over the past decade; such as finite-state based morphological analysers and generators in the GiellaLT repository (Moshagen et al., 2014), XML and MediaWiki based online dictionary (Rueter and Hämäläinen, 2017) and most recently a universal dependency treebank (Nivre et al., 2019). However, due to the pluricentric nature of the language (see (Rueter and Hämäläinen, 2019)), these tools are far from perfect. One of the core design principles of Ve′rdd is to bring these tools closer to non-technical community members editing a high-quality dictionary.

Building dictionaries is an essential part of resource creation when working on endangered low-resource languages. At the same time, lexical resources are an important part of the work done on computational morphological descriptions, such as finite state transducers. We argue that these lines of work have not traditionally entirely met each others. Traditionally the distinction may have been easier, as some dictionaries were intended to be printed, and others served computational infrastructure such as spell checkers. Nowadays, however, all dictionaries are born digital. Much of the dictionary writing work, often connected to traditional linguistic descriptions and the needs of the communities themselves, is still customarily done by hand using ordinary text processing software.

In other contexts, various other tools have been used. SIL FieldWorks (Baines, 2009) has been popular among many language documentation projects, although it clearly is not suitable for all projects and lacks many functionalities (Rogers, 2010). Commercial tool TLEx (Joffe and De Schryver, 2004) has also been used, although we personally would not prefer attempts at the use of commercial proprietary software in a language documentation context. These also all represent traditional, installed software that do not allow easy cooperation on a larger team level. A project that comes closer to our work is Lexonomy (Měchura,

---

[1]https://akusanat.com/verdd
Source code available: https://github.com/mokha/verdd

[2]Ve′rdd means stream in Skolt Sami

Proceedings of the 27th International Conference on Computational Linguistics, pages 1–6
Barcelona, Spain (Online), December 12, 2020.

2017). A central difference here is that our work connects the formal computational descriptions to the dictionary editing process, whereas other projects seem to principally offer a digital environment for the traditional dictionary making itself.

Besides editing dictionaries, one important purpose of Ve'rdd system is to allow combining information from different dictionaries. Many parts of lexical information that we want to present combines various sources. For example, etymological data by definition involves several dictionaries and their intercomparison. Similarly dialect dictionaries are inherently connected to the lexicons of their corresponding standard languages.

In many cases such specialized dictionaries may be practical to represent as distinct works, but still their connections to the other resources are myriad, and essential for the whole enterprise. Ve'rdd makes it possible to add these relationships between different entry and relation types. Resulting specialized dictionaries can, if wanted, be exported, but this way we avoid repeating the shared parts of the entries and can minimize duplicate efforts.

2 Ve'rdd System

In this section, we describe the major features implemented in Ve'rdd. Ve'rdd is developed in Python using Django framework. Django has been picked as it scores high when compared to other web frameworks in terms of quality attributes (Plekhanova, 2009).

When building Ve'rdd, modularity was constantly kept in mind to allow the system to be extended, incorporated into other systems or used for other languages. Currently, the system keeps track of the following elements in a dictionary: 1) lexemes, 2) their inflectional paradigms, 3) any relevant external links to them, 4) relations between two lexemes, 5) sources that backup these relations (e.g. other existing dictionaries), and 6) examples and 7) metadata to lexemes and relations. Nonetheless, we are considering adding dialectal transcriptions and locale information to lexemes, which, in addition to preserving this information, would support geolinguistics studies of these languages and facilitate developing computational models for processing dialects (c.f. (Partanen et al., 2019)).

Ve'rdd supports importing existing dictionaries in XML and CSV formats or from the Akusanat MediaWiki dictionary (Hämäläinen and Rueter, 2018) directly, this is to allow a smooth transition for editors to the tool without the need to input the data manually. In the import process, Ve'rdd takes care of wrong character encoding by mapping wrong variations into correct versions. This unification of characters is important as many of the special characters used in Skolt have either emerged in the Unicode standard recently, have wrong, similar looking Unicode characters or are impossible to type without an appropriate keyboard layout. This has lead to a high degree of inconsistencies of the characters used to write Skolt Sami, even if the text has been saved in UTF-8.

Figure 1 shows the front page of Ve'rdd, in which users can use the advanced search functionality to filter lexemes by lemma (fully, partially or matching a regular expression), language, source they appeared in, whether they have been verified and so on. Additionally, they can sort the result by their assonance and consonance which could help in discovering lexemes sharing an inflectional form. Users can access, edit or delete lexemes from this page. Furthermore, users can download the entire result of the search query or enter the bulk approving mode where they can tick a checkbox to confirm that the information associated with the lexeme is correct, which will highlight the approved lexemes in green as illustrated in the figure. A similar search interface also exists for relations.

Ve'rdd utilizes the Skolt FST (Rueter and Hämäläinen, 2020) through UralicNLP (Hämäläinen, 2019) to produce inflectional paradigms. The transducers are built on HFST (Lindén et al., 2013), which makes it easy to integrate transducers for other languages as well. The most common paradigms are displayed under the mini-paradigms section; nonetheless, users can access the full list of generated word inflections by clicking on the "See all miniparadigms" button. Users have the ability to add new inflectional forms and, in case of a wrong inflection produced by the transducers, they can correct it by adding a form that overwrites the wrong word form. Corrections of this nature are monitored closely and used as a feedback to update the transducers.

The system organizes the lexicographic data into a list of lexemes that contain all the relevant infor-

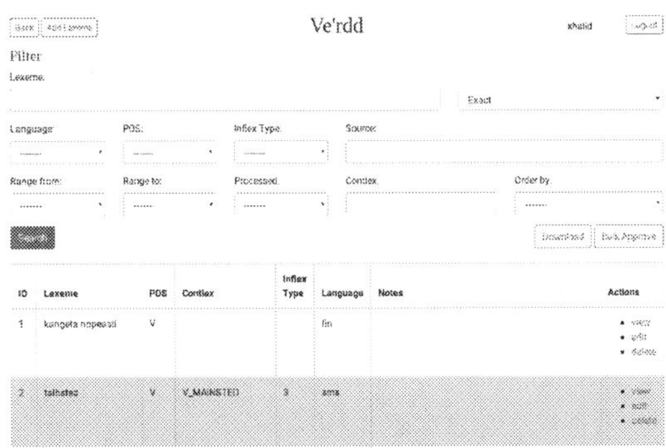

Figure 1: The advanced search interface for finding lexemes to be processed.

mation to the lexeme itself (such as inflection, language, part-of-speech) and relations in between two lexemes. The relations (such as derivations, compounds and translations) linked to a lexeme are also shown in the lexeme view interface. Sources (e.g. other dictionaries) that support the defined relation, along with example sentences and metadata that are specific to the relation, are presented alongside the relation. The sources functionality makes it possible to compare the different dictionaries that have been imported into the system.

Users can edit, delete or supply Ve′rdd with new information regarding any of its elements (e.g. lexemes, relations, sources . . . etc). Ve′rdd keeps track of all versions of instances along with who changed them and when, to mitigate introducing inaccurate information and losing the ability to revert back to the correct instances.

Once a user has finished checking or processing a lexeme, they can navigate to the next or previous lexeme using the navigation lists at the sides of the lexeme information. The navigation list depends on the search query the user defined during their filtering phase. This gives them the ability to move form a lexeme to another effortlessly without going back to the search results.

At the end of the editing period of the dictionary, approved relations are automatically exported by Ve′rdd into a LaTeX file, which are then included in a modular LaTeX dictionary template. The dictionary template is language independent and renders entries produced by Ve′rdd using predefined commands as a part of the template, which yields a full print-ready dictionary that is automatically generated. Editors can manually check and polish the entries to ensure that the document satisfies the editorial requirements set for publishing the dictionary.

3   Catering to the Language Community

Interaction with members of the language community in charge of editing the dictionary has been an important part of the project since its beginning. In this section, we describe the needs that were identified when discussing with the community members and observing their workflow.

3.1   Initial Requirements for the System

As a part of the project of editing a new version of the Finnish-Skolt Sami dictionary, a need for an editing system arose. Since dictionary editing for Skolt Sami has been done either with paper dictionaries in mind or with online dictionaries in mind (c.f. (Hämäläinen and Rueter, 2018)), a system with a user-interface and functionality supporting both modalities was needed.

Members of any given language community cannot be expected to have mastered language documentation, nor can they be expected to posses the technical skills needed to run command line applications for morphological analysers or edit XML-formatted dictionaries. The system should therefore provide a graphical user interface that can be used simultaneously by multiple non-technical dictionary editors.

An abstraction of the workflow is the following: the dictionary editors go through existing lexicographic resources imported into the system. They need to verify and correct each entry with the possibility of adding new entries when needed. As similar words behave in similar ways, the editors need a mechanism of filtering and sorting the words in the system based on similar vowels (assonance), consonants (consonance) and word ending. For this purpose, Ve'rdd has an extensive searching, filtering and sorting functionality.

As editors go through the lexical entries in the system, a history of changes should be kept. Ve'rdd includes a special administrator view that shows all the edits done in the system and their respective editors. Edits can be reverted back for individual words or individual relations without the need of reverting anything more than necessary.

Finally, the system should be able to output its data in meaningful formats. This means outputting the final dictionary for printing, a CSV and XML. Some of the dictionary editors are familiar with Excel and they have a need to see the data in a format compatible with the software. Then again, some more technical users are interested in XML for using it for NLP.

The workflow anticipated in the XML, Akusanat and even Ve'rdd have, at times, proven to be incompatible with those of the actual native users. This may be the result of experience with pencil and paper approaches to language documentation. Some of the users have been more familiar with ticking translation pairs off in a long list (all on paper first and then on Ve'rdd). For this reason we organised sessions with the community members to better understand their needs.

3.2 First User Session

The first session with the participating community members was organized in Inari in the Finnish Lapland. Two native Skolt Sami speakers and one non-native Skolt Sami teacher who are to edit the dictionary participated in the tutorial session. The purpose was to get to know better how they do dictionary editing and more concretely what their needs are. This session revealed that several key features were lacking and that the user interface needed more refining for a better usability.

The development language of Ve'rdd has been English and therefore the user interface was initially in English. The community members demanded it be localized in Finnish as they are not fluent enough in English to use the system. Another interface problem was that the community members needed a quick visual way of seeing which words and relations they had already verified. Although the system kept track of this already, this was made visually clearer by coloring the words and relations that had already been verified entirely in light green.

By observing how the system was used, we quickly noticed that the editors were consulting several different pages to get their work done. They used Akusanat[3] to see the full inflectional paradigms of the Skolt Sami words. Ve'rdd initially included only a miniparadigm that highlighted only the linguistically meaningful inflections. As the community members are no linguists, however, they felt a need to see the entire full inflection paradigms. This feature was automatically introduced in Ve'rdd by inflecting the words with UralicNLP. Simultaneously a feature for editing the paradigms was also introduced in case the FSTs were producing incorrect inflectional forms.

Another website the editors consulted was Sami TermWiki[4], which contains a list of terms that have been established as the official recommendations by the Sámi Giellagáldu institution. We collected the Skol Sami terms from the Sami TermWiki and added them to Ve'rdd. For the words that are recommended by Sámi Giellagáldu, a link to TermWiki appears in Ve'rdd.

Two new relation types were requested by the community members. First, they needed to keep some words in the dictionary, although they are not recommended forms, but they need to be kept for the sake of completeness with a reference to the normative form. This relation type was introduced as alternative form relation. Furthermore, there was a wish to link derivational forms to the word they derived from. This was done automatically with the GiellaLT transducers in UralicNLP. We processed all the words in the system and linked the ones that received a derivational morphological reading with a matching lemma and part-of-speech.

3.3 Second User Session

The second user session was arranged over Skype with two language community members, a student and the instructor of the dictionary project. In this session, it became evident that the editors had resorted to a

---

4

more traditional Finnish lexicographic approach, i.e. doing editorial work in a pencil and paper fashion. In keeping with this tradition, the three editors had been directed to inspect lists of Skolt Sami verbs with their Finnish translations by their instructor, head editor.

This workflow, although counter-intuitive from the tool developers' perspective, sits well with the editors. In fact, it is difficult to entice them to use the Ve′rdd tool directly; since the previous session only 28 entries with all relations had been approved. Needless to say, another set of printed word lists was requested. The editors preferred a list of words on paper to individual words, one at a time. As one of the editors described it: "When I pack my suitcase, I don't put in one individual thing at a time, so I don't feel good about dealing with words on an individual basis." This, in fact, illustrates the practice where editors want to deal with one set of words at a time, i.e. there might be a part-of-speech constraint or even features of assonance or consonance utilized in the sorting of several words for bulk approval in a dictionary editing system.

We recognized the alignment of linguistic and first language user intuition. While a linguistic approach to inflection type categorization might include bulk assessment of similar assonance or consonance, the native language speakers were also looking for word form associations. For this reason we decided there had to be an easy way to print out a list of source-language and target-language word pairs; a structure which could also be realized as paired words with an adjacent column of tick boxes as well a columns for identification of the individual relation. This latter feature could then be used with feeding the results of pencil-n-paper inspections of translation, derivation and etymology relations. This interface design decision is meant to mimic the experience they would have when using a pencil and a paper, although by using a flat design paradigm as opposed to a fully skeuomorphic design, as there is evidence of the former resulting in a higher perceived usability (Spiliotopoulos et al., 2018).

A second feature requested was the ability to add relations more freely to a newly added lemma in addition to simple translation relation. This requires exposing the features stored in the relation information to an editable form in the user interface.

4 Future Directions and Discussion

In this paper, we have presented Ve′rdd, a dictionary editing system for Skolt Sami. Our system relies on technologies that exist in the exact same format for multiple minority languages in the GiellaLT system. This means that the system can readily be used with a little to no configuration just by adding a new language code from the list of 32 languages currently supported by UralicNLP.

Currently, the system is capable of automatically generating morphological inflections, and these inflectional forms can be edited together with the continuation lexicon information. In other words, this can be used to fix any issues that are present in the FSTs. However, at the moment, this is a manual endeavor. Whenever the inflectional forms are edited, the person in charge of writing the FSTs can see the edits in the administration view of Ve′rdd and adjust the FSTs accordingly. A future solution would be to make it possible to inspect and edit FSTs directly in the system, similarly to the system proposed by (Lepp et al., 2019).

As a longer term goal for the system is a closer integration with the GiellaLT infrastructure and Akusanat MediaWiki dictionary. Ve′rdd currently uses the tools and lexicographic information coming from these systems, but any edits made in Ve′rdd do not get reflected back to the other systems. As the focus is currently in finalizing the printed Skolt Sami dictionary, this bi-directionality has been left for the future.

The development of Ve′rdd continues in close collaboration with the Skolt Sami language community. The immediate next step is to come into an agreement on the layout of the final paper dictionary. Currently, Ve′rdd does support outputting the lexicographic data into a LaTeX template that can be edited before the final PDF version. However, the actual final layout is to be decided.

References

Khalid Alnajjar, Mika Hämäläinen, and Jack Rueter. 2020. On editing dictionaries for uralic languages in an online environment. In *Proceedings of the Sixth International Workshop on Computational Linguistics of Uralic Languages*, pages 26–30.

David Baines. 2009. Fieldworks language explorer (flex). *eLEX2009*.

Mika Hämäläinen. 2019. UralicNLP: An NLP library for Uralic languages. *Journal of Open Source Software*, 4(37):1345.

Mika Hämäläinen and Jack Rueter. 2018. Advances in Synchronized XML-MediaWiki Dictionary Development in the Context of Endangered Uralic Languages. In *Proceedings of the Eighteenth EURALEX International Congress*, pages 967–978.

David Joffe and Gilles-Maurice De Schryver. 2004. Tshwanelex: a state-of-the-art dictionary compilation program. In *11th EURALEX International Congress (EURALEX-2004)*, pages 99–104. Faculté des Lettres et des Sciences Humaines.

Haley Lepp, Olga Zamaraeva, and Emily M. Bender. 2019. Visualizing inferred morphotactic systems. In *Proceedings of the 2019 Conference of the North American Chapter of the Association for Computational Linguistics (Demonstrations)*, pages 127–131, Minneapolis, Minnesota, June. Association for Computational Linguistics.

Krister Lindén, Erik Axelson, Senka Drobac, Sam Hardwick, Juha Kuokkala, Jyrki Niemi, Tommi A Pirinen, and Miikka Silfverberg. 2013. Hfst—a system for creating nlp tools. In *International workshop on systems and frameworks for computational morphology*, pages 53–71. Springer.

Michal Měchura. 2017. Introducing lexonomy: an open-source dictionary writing and publishing system. In *Electronic Lexicography in the 21st Century: Lexicography from Scratch. Proceedings of the eLex 2017 conference*, pages 19–21.

Christopher Moseley, editor. 2010. *Atlas of the World's Languages in Danger*. UNESCO Publishing, 3rd edition. Online version: http://www.unesco.org/languages-atlas/.

Sjur Moshagen, Jack Rueter, Tommi Pirinen, Trond Trosterud, and Francis M. Tyers. 2014. Open-Source Infrastructures for Collaborative Work on Under-Resourced Languages. In *The LREC 2014 Workshop "CCURL 2014 - Collaboration and Computing for Under-Resourced Languages in the Linked Open Data Era"*, pages 71–77.

Joakim Nivre, Dan Zeman, Markus Juutinen, Jack Rueter, Mika Hämäläinen, and Francis M. Tyers. 2019. Ud_skolt_sami-giellagas, 11. Published by LINDAT/CLARIN digital library at the Institute of Formal and Applied Linguistics (ÚFAL), Faculty of Mathematics and Physics, Charles University.

Niko Partanen, Mika Hämäläinen, and Khalid Alnajjar. 2019. Dialect text normalization to normative standard finnish. In Wei Xu, Alan Ritter, Tim Baldwin, and Afshin Rahimi, editors, *The Fifth Workshop on Noisy User-generated Text (W-NUT 2019)*, page 141–146, United States. The Association for Computational Linguistics.

Julia Plekhanova. 2009. Evaluating web development frameworks: Django, ruby on rails and cakephp. *Institute for Business and Information Technology*.

Chris Rogers. 2010. Review of fieldworks language explorer (flex) 3.0. *Language Documentation & Conservation*, 4:78–84.

Jack Michael Rueter and Mika Hämäläinen. 2017. Synchronized mediawiki based analyzer dictionary development. In *3rd International Workshop for Computational Linguistics of Uralic Languages Proceedings of the Workshop*. Association for Computational Linguistics.

Jack Rueter and Mika Hämäläinen. 2019. Skolt sami, the makings of a pluricentric language, where does it stand? In Rudolf Muhr, Josep Angel Mas Castells, and Jack Rueter, editors, *European Pluricentric Languages in Contact and Conflict*, Bern, Switzerland. Peter Lang.

Jack Rueter and Mika Hämäläinen. 2020. Fst morphology for the endangered skolt sami language. In *Proceedings of the 1st Joint Workshop on Spoken Language Technologies for Under-resourced languages (SLTU) and Collaboration and Computing for Under-Resourced Languages (CCURL)*, pages 250–257.

Konstantinos Spiliotopoulos, Maria Rigou, and Spiros Sirmakessis. 2018. A comparative study of skeuomorphic and flat design from a ux perspective. *Multimodal Technologies and Interaction*, 2(2):31.

MaintNet: A Collaborative Open-Source Library for Predictive Maintenance Language Resources

Farhad Akhbardeh, Travis Desell, Marcos Zampieri
Rochester Institute of Technology, United States
`{fa3019, tjdvse, mazgla}@rit.edu`

Abstract

Maintenance record logbooks are an emerging text type in NLP. An important part of them typically consist of free text with many domain specific technical terms, abbreviations, and non-standard spelling and grammar. This poses difficulties for NLP pipelines trained on standard corpora. Analyzing and annotating such documents is of particular importance in the development of predictive maintenance systems, which aim to improve operational efficiency, reduce costs, prevent accidents, and save lives. In order to facilitate and encourage research in this area, we have developed MaintNet, a collaborative open-source library of technical and domain-specific language resources. MaintNet provides novel logbook data from the aviation, automotive, and facility maintenance domains along with tools to aid in their (pre-)processing and clustering. Furthermore, it provides a way to encourage discussion on and sharing of new datasets and tools for logbook data analysis.

1 Introduction

With the rapid development of information technologies, engineering systems are generating increasing amounts of data that are used by various industries to improve their products. Maintenance records are one such type of data. They typically consist of event logbooks which are collected in many domains such as aviation, transportation, and healthcare (Tanguy et al., 2016; Altuncu et al., 2018). The analysis of maintenance records is particularly important in the development of predictive maintenance systems, which can be used to prevent accidents and reduce maintenance costs (Jarry et al., 2018).

Maintenance record datasets generally contain free text fields describing issues (or problems) written in non-standard language with many abbreviations and domain specific terms, as in the instances presented in Table 1.

ID	Job Code	Report Date	Problem
211052	7130	8/28/2012	DOING MX PERFORM T/O @ 3200, MP WON'T GO ANY HIGHER THAN 24
221313	7200	4/7/2015	FRONT R/H BAFFLE WORN THROUGH FROM MUFFLER SHROUD NEED NEW BFFLE.
211585	550	4/10/2015	LACING CORD LOOSE ON SCAT TUBING + IGN LEAD TO FRAME, R/H SI, NEED @ ENG #2.
221958	7250	4/11/2016	ROUGH RUNNING ENG ON START. ENGINE RAN SMOOTHER AS IT WAR
221646	7230	4/20/2016	DURING IDLE CHECK ON RUN UP, ENGINE QUIT. RESTART ENGINE & Q

Table 1: Five sample of Maintnet's aviation dataset.

Standard NLP tools, however, are typically trained on standard contemporary corpora (e.g. newspaper texts). They struggle when dealing with the domain specific terminology, abbreviations, and non-standard spelling which are abundant in maintenance records. To help encourage further study in this

Proceedings of the 27th International Conference on Computational Linguistics, pages 7–11
Barcelona, Spain (Online), December 12, 2020.

area, we present MaintNet[1], a collaborative, open-source library for technical language resources with a special focus on predictive maintenance data.

The main contributions of this paper are the following:

1. The development of MaintNet, a user-friendly web-based platform that serves as a repository hosting a variety of resources and tools developed to process predictive maintenance and technical logbook data.

2. The creation of several important language resources for technical language and predictive maintenance such as abbreviation lists, morphosyntactic information lists, and termbanks for the aviation, automotive, and facility maintenance domains. All these resources as well as raw data from these domains are made freely available to the research community via MaintNet.

3. The development of several novel Python packages for (pre-)processing technical language which we make available to the research community. This includes stop word removal, stemmers, lemmatizers, POS tagging, document clustering, and more.

4. A collaborative environment in which the community can contribute with data and resources and interact with developers and other members of the community via forums.

2 MaintNet Features

2.1 Language Resources

To the best of our knowledge, there are no freely available tools and libraries developed to process such data, which makes MaintNet a unique resource. MaintNet currently features datasets from the aviation, automotive, and facilities domains (see Table 2), and it will be expanded with the collaboration of the interested members of the NLP community working on similar topics.

Domain	Dataset	Instances	Tokens	Source
Automotive	Maintenance	617	4,443	Connecticut Open Data
	Accident	54,367	242,012	NYS Department of Motor Vehicles
Aviation	Maintenance	6,169	76,866	University of North Dakota Aviation Program
	Accident	5,268	162,533	Open Data by Socrata
Facility	Maintenance	87,276	2,469,003	Baltimore City Maryland Preventive Maintenance

Table 2: The number of instances and tokens in each dataset/domain.

Predictive maintenance datasets are hard to obtain due to the sensitive information they contain. Therefore, we work closely with the data providers to ensure that any confidential and sensitive information in the dataset remains anonymous. In addition to the datasets, MaintNet further provides the user with domain specific abbreviation dictionaries, morphosyntactic annotation, and term banks. The abbreviation dictionaries contains abbreviated validated by domain experts. The morphosyntactic annotation contains the part of speech (POS) tag, compound, lemma, and word stems. Finally, the domain term banks contain the collected list of terms that are used in each domain along with a sample of usage in the corpus.

2.2 Pre-processing and Tools

Grouping maintenance issues by time is an important step in the analysis of logbook data. Most of the predictive maintenance datasets available, however, do not feature the reason for maintenance or the category of the issues making it impossible to train classification systems on such systems. To address this problem, we implemented several (pre-)processing steps to clean and extract information from logbooks aiming at document clustering and classification. The complete processing pipeline is shown in Figure 1.

The pre-processing steps start with text normalization, lowercasing, stop word and punctuation removal. Then we treat special characters with NLTK's (Bird et al., 2009) regular expression library,

---

[1]Available at: `https://people.rit.edu/fa3019/MaintNet/`

followed by stemming (Snowball Stemmer), lemmatization (WordNet (Miller, 1992)), and tokenization (NLTK tokenizer). POS annotation is carried out using the NLTK POS tagger. Finally, Term frequency-inverse document frequency (TF-IDF) is obtained using the *gensim tfidf model* (Rehurek and Sojka, 2010).

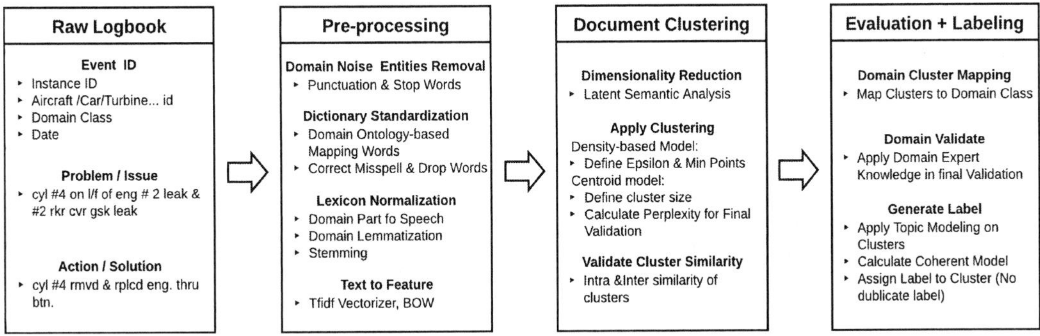

Figure 1: A pipeline of pre-processing and information extraction of maintenance dataset in MaintNet.

To address misspellings and abbreviations which are abundant in predictive maintenance datasets, we explored various state-of-the-art spellcheckers including Enchant[2], Pyspellchecker[3], Symspellpy[4], and Autocorrect[5]. We also developed our own spell checker using Levenshtein distance (Aggarwal and Zhai, 2012) where a dictionary of domain specific words is used to map the misspelling candidates to words in the dictionary. The Levenshtein algorithm was chosen over other distance metrics (*e.g.*, Euclidian, Cosine) as it allows us to control the minimum number of string edits. The performance of our method compared to other spellcheckers in a sub set of the aviation dataset is presented in Table 3.

Total Number of Documents		500
Tokens		3299
Non-standard		289
	Enchant	84
	PySpellchecker	61
Success Rate (%)	Autocorrect	73
	Levenshtein	98

Table 3: Results of the spelling correction and abbreviation expansion methods in terms of success rate.

In MaintNet we also developed document clustering systems customized to logbook data and we make the scripts available to the community. As previously stated, logbook datasets are often not annotated with issue categories requiring a domain expert to group instances into categories. Here we use clustering methods to help grouping documents together.

We first convert tokens into a numerical representation using *tfidfvectorizer* (ElSahar et al., 2017) and we obtain a large matrix of document terms (DT). We used truncated singular value decomposition (SVD) (ElSahar et al., 2017) known as latent semantic analysis (LSA), to perform dimensionality reduction. We then experimented with four clustering techniques: k-means (Jain, 2010), Density-Based Spatial Clustering of Applications with Noise (DBSCAN) (Ester et al., 1996), Latent Dirichlet Analysis (LDA) (Vorontsov et al., 2015), and hierarchical clustering (Aggarwal and Zhai, 2012). DBSCAN and hierarchical clustering do not require a predetermined number of clusters. For k-means, silhouette and inertia (Fraley and Raftery, 1998) were used to determine the number of clusters while perplexity (Fraley and Raftery, 1998) and coherence (Vorontsov et al., 2015) scores were used for LDA.

---

[2]https://www.abisource.com/projects/enchant/
[3]https://github.com/barrust/pyspellchecker
[4]https://github.com/wolfgarbe/SymSpell
[5]https://github.com/fsondej/autocorrect

Finally, we use three different similarity algorithms: Levenshtein, Jaro, and cosine (Fraley and Raftery, 1998) to calculate intra- and inter-cluster similarity. Cosine similarity is commonly used and is independent of the length of document, while Jaro is more flexible by providing a rating of matching strings. We collected human annotated instances by a domain expert to serve as our gold standard, and these are provided on MaintNet to encourage research into improving unsupervised clustering of maintenance logbooks.

2.3 Community Participation

MaintNet provides various webpages for users to communicate with each other and the project developers; as well as upload data to share with the community (see Figure 2). We hope this will help further facilitate discussion and research in this important and under explored area.

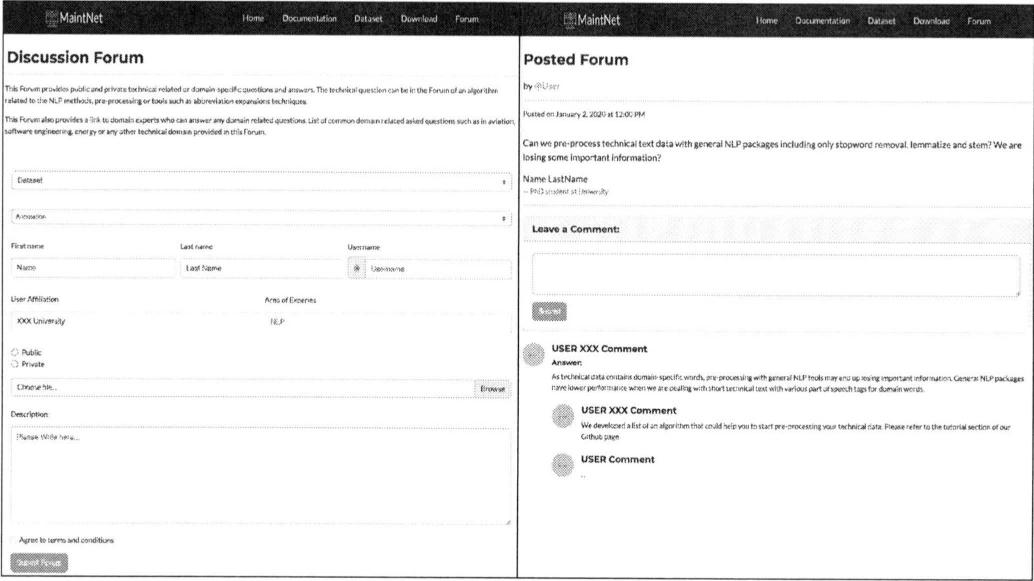

Figure 2: A screenshot of MaintNet's discussion webpages.

3 Conclusions and Future Work

In this paper we presented MaintNet, a collaborative open-source library for predictive maintenance language resources. MaintNet provides raw technical logbook data as well as several language resources such as abbreviation lists, morphosyntactic information lists, and termbanks from the aviation, automotive and facilities domains. Tools developed in Python are also made available for pre-processing, such as spell checking, POS tagging, and document clustering. In addition to these tools, the collaborative aspects of MaintNet should be emphasized. We welcome the community to contribute with new datasets that can be processed using the tools available at MaintNet, or share new and improved tools developed with MaintNet's open source data.

MaintNet is also expanding as current work involves processing data from additional domains such as healthcare and power systems (*e.g.*, wind turbines). These datasets will be made available on MaintNet in upcoming months. We also aim to collect and release datasets and tools for languages other than English in the near future.

Acknowledgments

We would like to thank Rachael Thormann for the voiceover video. We further thank the University of North Dakota aviation program for the aviation maintenance records dataset and Zechariah Morgain for evaluating the results of the pre-processing and clustering algorithms.

References

Charu C. Aggarwal and ChengXiang Zhai. 2012. A survey of text clustering algorithms. In *Mining Text Data*.

M. Tarik Altuncu, Erik Mayer, Sophia N. Yaliraki, and Mauricio Barahona. 2018. From text to topics in healthcare records: An unsupervised graph partitioning methodology. *ArXiv*, abs/1807.02599.

Steven Bird, Ewan Klein, and Edward Loper. 2009. *Natural Language Processing with Python*. O'Reilly.

Hady ElSahar, Elena Demidova, Simon Gottschalk, Christophe Gravier, and Frédérique Laforest. 2017. Unsupervised open relation extraction. *ArXiv*, abs/1801.07174.

Martin Ester, Hans-Peter Kriegel, Jörg Sander, and Xiaowei Xu. 1996. A density-based algorithm for discovering clusters in large spatial databases with noise. In *KDD*.

Chris Fraley and Adrian E. Raftery. 1998. How many clusters? which clustering method? answers via model-based cluster analysis. *Comput. J.*, 41:578–588.

Anil Kumar Jain. 2010. Data clustering: 50 years beyond k-means. *Pattern Recognition Letters*, 31:651–666.

Gabriel Jarry, Daniel Delahaye, Florence Nicol, and Eric Feron. 2018. Aircraft atypical approach detection using functional principal component analysis. In *SID*.

George A. Miller. 1992. Wordnet: A lexical database for english. *Commun. ACM*, 38:39–41.

Radim Rehurek and Petr Sojka. 2010. Software framework for topic modelling with large corpora. In *LREC*.

Ludovic Tanguy, Nikola Tulechki, Assaf Urieli, Eric Hermann, and Céline Raynal. 2016. Natural language processing for aviation safety reports: From classification to interactive analysis. *Computers in Industry*, 78:80–95.

Konstantin Vorontsov, Oleksandr Frei, Murat Apishev, Peter Romov, and Marina Dudarenko. 2015. Bigartm: Open source library for regularized multimodal topic modeling of large collections. In *AIST*.

DART: A Lightweight Quality-Suggestive Data-to-Text Annotation Tool

†**Ernie Chang**, †**Jeriah Caplinger**, *__Alex Marin__, †**Xiaoyu Shen**, †**Vera Demberg**
†Dept. of Language Science and Technology, Saarland University
{cychang,jeriahc,xiaoyu,vera}@coli.uni-saarland.de
*Microsoft Corporation, Redmond, WA
{alemari}@microsoft.com

Abstract

We present a lightweight annotation tool, the *Data AnnotatoR Tool (DART)*, for the general task of labeling structured data with textual descriptions. The tool is implemented as an interactive application that reduces human efforts in annotating large quantities of structured data, *e.g.* in the format of a table or tree structure. By using a backend sequence-to-sequence model, our system iteratively analyzes the annotated labels in order to better sample unlabeled data. In a simulation experiment performed on annotating large quantities of structured data, *DART* has been shown to reduce the total number of annotations needed with active learning and automatically suggesting relevant labels.

1 Introduction

Neural data-to-text generation has been the subject of much research in recent years (Gkatzia, 2016). Traditionally, the task takes as input structured data which comes in the form of tables with attribute and value pairs, and generates free-form, human-readable text.

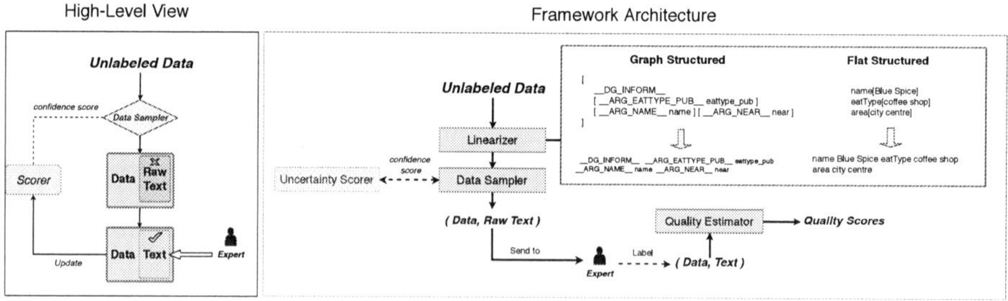

Figure 1: Left: Overview of the DART toolkit usage. Right: Diagram of the framework architecture.

Past example datasets include Restaurants (Wen et al., 2015) or graph-structure inputs (Balakrishnan et al., 2019). Analogously, most conversation systems (Williams et al., 2015; Crook et al., 2018) utilize intermediate meaning representation (data) as input to generate natural language sentences. In practice, however, these systems are highly reliant on the use of large-scale labeled data. Each new domain requires additional annotations to pair the new data with matching text. With the rise in development of natural language generation (NLG) systems from structured data, there is also an increased need for annotation tools that reduce labeling time and effort for constructing complex sentence labels. Unlike other labeling tasks, such as sequence tagging (Lin et al., 2019), where the labels are non-complex and correspond to fixed sets of classes, data-to-text generation entails providing complete sentence labels for each data instance. To construct textual description is time-consuming and therefore it can be beneficial for the system to automatically suggest texts and allow the annotators to accept or *partially correct* them. To this end, we propose to create an interactive annotation tool: Data AnnotatoR Tool (DART[1]) that

[1]Demo is available at https://youtu.be/onPUgQ2ixpI

Proceedings of the 27th International Conference on Computational Linguistics, pages 12–17
Barcelona, Spain (Online), December 12, 2020.

System	Label Types	Programming Language	Has Label Recommendation ?	User Interface	Use Active Learning ?
DART	Text	Python	✓	GUI	✓
AlpacaTag (Lin et al., 2019)	Tag	Python	✓	GUI	✓
YEDDA (Yang et al., 2018)	Tag	Python	✓	GUI	✗

Table 1: A general comparison of relevant GUI-based annotation tools.

reduces structured data-to-text annotation efforts by incorporating *automatic label suggestion* and the *uncertainty-based active learning algorithm* (Lewis and Catlett, 1994; Culotta and McCallum, 2004). *DART* serves as a natural complement to downstream data-to-text systems, rather than an end-to-end NLG system. As such, it can assist in the development of both traditional rule-based systems (*e.g.* (Reiter, 2007)), and the recent neural systems (*e.g.* (Balakrishnan et al., 2019; Chang et al., 2020; Shen et al., 2020; Hong et al., 2019)).

As a lightweight, standalone desktop application, *DART* can be easily distributed to domain experts and installed on local devices. *DART* consists of a user-friendly interface that allows experts to iteratively improve the overall corpus quality with partial corrections. Overall, the toolkit provides three advantages: (1) It reduces labeling difficulty by automatically providing natural language label recommendations; (2) It efficiently solicits data for which it has low confidence (or high uncertainty) in its generated text to be annotated, so that overall annotation efforts can be reduced; (3) Lastly, it provides real-time in-progress updates with statistics about the labeled corpus as to help direct the overall annotation process. This is achieved with a myriad of quality estimators that assess corpus diversity and the overall text quality.

2 Annotation Framework

DART is a desktop application built with PyQt5[2]. It is compiled into a single executable with PyInstaller[3], a tool that supports both Mac OS and Windows environments. It contains an intuitive interface as described in section 3. Annotation experts interact with *DART* in the following way: (1) A file containing unlabeled data is uploaded. (2) The system samples some data instances from the file, with a selection strategy based on signals from the sequence-to-sequence *uncertainty scorer* (section 2.1) and performed with the *data sampler* (section 2.2). (3) Experts then annotate the provided data by correcting the suggested labels (available after the first iteration of (1)-(2)). (4) During the process of annotation, the labeled corpus quality is indicated by the annotation *quality estimators* (section 2.3) for experts to determine if the process were to be terminated. We discuss each component in more detail below.

2.1 Uncertainty Scorer

We represent the structured unannotated corpus as $D = d_{i=1}^N$ where each data sample d_i comprises of a token sequence linearized from underlying structured data samples x_i, as motivated by past works in the multilingual surface realization tasks (Mille et al., 2018). We employ the Transformer-based (Vaswani et al., 2017) encoder-decoder architecture as the sequence-to-sequence model. The sequences d_i are fed into the model in order to generate a text sequence $t_i = w_1, w_2, ..., w_{M_i}$ of length M_i.

Since the model is given only the input data d, we compute reconstruction scores for this data, and use the cross-entropy loss as the *uncertainty score*. To do so, we perform round-trip training[4] where the source data is reconstructed to achieve *cycle consistency*. In this setup, the same encoder and decoder are used in both forward and backward training *i.e.* a forward model $M_{forward}$ goes from data to text and the backward model $M_{backward}$ converts the text back into data. We define the round-trip training log-loss as the uncertainty score $S_{uncertainty}$ (as Eq. 1a) where $\mathcal{L}(\cdot)$ is the cross-entropy loss. d' is the

---

[2]https://riverbankcomputing.com/software/pyqt/intro
[3]https://www.pyinstaller.org/
[4]Defined in (Lample et al., 2017) as the back-translation technique where input data is reconstructed with $M_{forward}$ and $M_{backward}$ to compute consistency loss.

generated data using $M_{forward}$ and $M_{backward}$ given input data d.

$$\mathcal{S}_{\text{uncertainty}} = \mathbb{E}_{d \sim p_{\text{data}}(D)} \mathcal{L}\left(d', d\right) \tag{1a}$$

Next, we discuss how $\mathcal{S}_{uncertainty}$ is used in *uncertainty sampling* during data selection.

2.2 Data Sampler

The process of data selection identifies N data instances to be labeled such that the overall generation quality is improved. This can be achieved by learning the structure over data D (Tosh and Dasgupta, 2018). We adopt a simple technique to represent each data instance d as a bag-of-word (BOW) vector and further divide each *attribute-type* (first layer) into k clusters (*sub-type*, second layer) with the K-means algorithm[5] (Alsabti et al., 1997), which splits data instances into k clusters based on selected centroids.

We first rank the order of batch-size samples within each *sub-type* using *uncertainty scores* (in section 2.1) so that experts can annotate the ones with the least confident scores first. At sampling time, we obtain unlabeled data instances from all *sub-types* across all *attribute-types* iteratively. One sample is obtained from each *sub-type* before moving on to the next *sub-type*.

For data presented to be labeled, the system also suggests labels in order to reduce annotation efforts. *DART* employs a simple retrieval-based technique to obtain a text label t for each data instance d. Using the BOW representation of d, we simply find the most similar d' (cosine similarity) in the labeled pool of (d_i, t_i) pairs, and use its text label t_i as the suggestion[6]. The sampling process continues until either all data instances are labeled or a satisfactory threshold value is reached for the quality metric on the labeled corpus (as defined in section 2.3).

2.3 Quality Estimator

To better manage the annotation process, we include the diversity metrics used in (Balakrishnan et al., 2019): *number of unique tokens, number of unique trigrams, Shannon token entropy, conditional bigram entropy*. Following (Novikova et al., 2016), we also measure various types of lexical richness including *type-token ratio (TTR)* and *Mean Segmental TTR (MSTTR)* (Lu, 2012), where higher values of TTR and MSTTR correspond to more diverse corpus. *DART* displays these scores on the *Status Display* as shown in Figure 2. These scores serve as on-the-fly quality estimates that help experts decide when sufficient labels have been collected.

3 User Interface

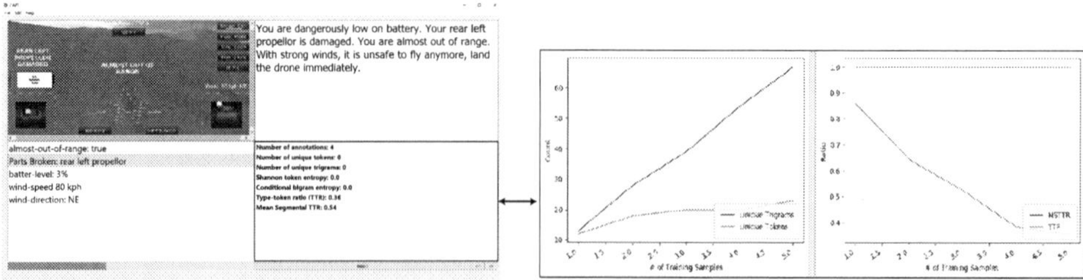

Figure 2: Screenshot of sample annotation interface showing the provided data, and the text box for annotation. On the bottom right, user can select either the statistics or plots indicating the corpus diversity and annotation count.

The interactive interface divides the interactive application window into a few compartments: *DART* includes a configuration editor interface that allows the experts to modify the delimiter (*e.g.* ",") between *attribute:value* pairs. For graph structured input, the delimiter (*e.g.* "__") is used to identify the attribute

---

[5]Using the implemented version from https://scikit-learn.org

[6]There are no suggestions for the initial batch of annotations.

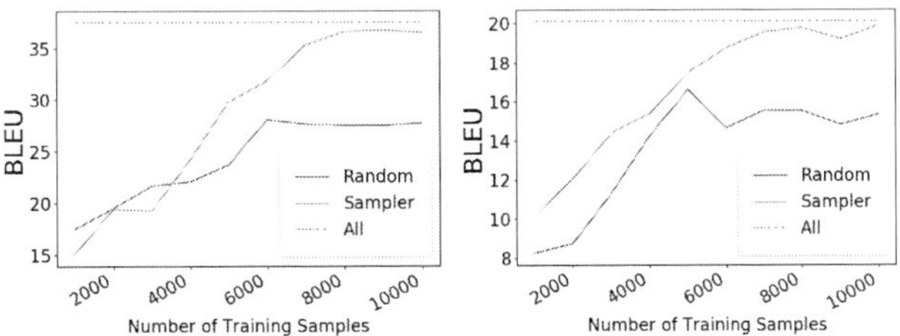

Figure 3: Performance comparison between DART's **data sampler**, **random sampling**, and retrieving labels from the full dataset (**ALL**) on E2E (Left) and the Weather (Right) datasets (42k data instances for E2E and 32k for weather), using the same retrieval method.

tags instead. Note that the system supports three granularity of tokenization: (1) word, (2) character, and (3) byte-pair encoding (BPE) (Sennrich et al., 2016). The top half of Figure 2 shows the main annotation page where experts can input constructed sentences into the text boxes based on suggested texts and the provided image (or short clip) [7]. As the expert annotates, the progress bar below the text box indicates when the background *uncertainty scorer* training session will begin. The bottom half of Figure 2 shows the annotation progress statistics, including the percentage of data types that have been annotated and the quality of overall templates. When a specified number of annotations has been created, experts can download both the annotated data samples along with data with predicted labels. In general, a high-quality corpus maintain a high corpus diversity (*e.g.* a MSTTR score of 0.75 or TTR of 0.01 in the E2E dataset (Novikova et al., 2016)) even as the number of annotation increases.

4 Experiments

Data. We use two different types of structured data: (A) Attribute-value pairs as used in the crowd-sourced *E2E* dataset (Novikova et al., 2017), and (B) the graph-structured data as defined in (Balakr-ishnan et al., 2019) on the *weather* domain. To simulate the annotation process, we employ the given training, development and test sets of each datasets for annotation tool evaluation, with the test set kept fixed. This amounts to roughly 42k samples for E2E and 32k for the weather training sets.

Simulation Study. To evaluate the effectiveness of *DART*, we perform a simulated experiment for each of our two datasets, E2E and Weather. We simulate the labeling process using both the retrieval-based method (**Sampler**, as discussed in section 2.2) and the baseline approach using random selection of data (**Random**) and compare the performance of the two methods relative to using the full dataset (**All**).

Results for the two datasets, E2E and Weather, are presented in Figure 3. On both datasets, the data sampler allows the retriever to obtain the same performance (*i.e.* with similar BLEU score as *ALL*) using only 10k labeled data instances, which is significantly less than that of the original dataset (*i.e.* 42k for *E2E* and 32k for *Weather*). As such, the number of required annotations to arrive at the same performance using all labeled data is significantly reduced for both datasets, to one-fifth of the original dataset size. In contrast, performance obtained using the *Random* selection is significantly worse (on the order of 6 to 10 BLEU points lower than the baseline) compared to using the *Sampler* selection while matching the number of training samples.

5 Conclusions

While a wide range of annotation tools for NLP tasks exists, most of these tools are targeted at non-textual labels. *DART* is designed to enable the ease of annotation where the labels are textual descriptions and the inputs are structured data. This is the initial version of the tool, and we hope to extend it to include a web-based version and to expand its functionality in the following ways: (1) support different types of encoders, and (2) improve upon the data sampling process.

---

[7]The use of pictures is shown to elicit better data (Novikova et al., 2016)

Acknowledgements

This research was funded in part by the German Research Foundation (DFG) as part of SFB 248 "Foundations of Perspicuous Software Systems". We sincerely thank the anonymous reviewers for their insightful comments that helped us to improve this paper.

References

Khaled Alsabti, Sanjay Ranka, and Vineet Singh. 1997. An efficient k-means clustering algorithm.

Anusha Balakrishnan, Jinfeng Rao, Kartikeya Upasani, Michael White, and Rajen Subba. 2019. Constrained decoding for neural NLG from compositional representations in task-oriented dialogue. In *Proceedings of the 57th Annual Meeting of the Association for Computational Linguistics*, pages 831–844, Florence, Italy, July. Association for Computational Linguistics.

Ernie Chang, David Ifeoluwa Adelani, Xiaoyu Shen, and Vera Demberg. 2020. Unsupervised pidgin text generation by pivoting english data and self-training. *arXiv preprint arXiv:2003.08272*.

Paul A Crook, Alex Marin, Vipul Agarwal, Samantha Anderson, Ohyoung Jang, Aliasgar Lanewala, Karthik Tangirala, and Imed Zitouni. 2018. Conversational semantic search: Looking beyond web search, q&a and dialog systems. In *Proceedings of the Eleventh ACM International Conference on Web Search and Data Mining*, pages 763–766. ACM.

Aron Culotta and Andrew McCallum. 2004. Confidence estimation for information extraction. In *Proceedings of HLT-NAACL 2004: Short Papers*, pages 109–112. Association for Computational Linguistics.

Dimitra Gkatzia. 2016. Content selection in data-to-text systems: A survey. *arXiv preprint arXiv:1610.08375*.

Xudong Hong, Ernie Chang, and Vera Demberg. 2019. Improving language generation from feature-rich tree-structured data with relational graph convolutional encoders. In *Proceedings of the 2nd Workshop on Multilingual Surface Realisation (MSR 2019)*, pages 75–80.

Guillaume Lample, Alexis Conneau, Ludovic Denoyer, and Marc'Aurelio Ranzato. 2017. Unsupervised machine translation using monolingual corpora only. *arXiv preprint arXiv:1711.00043*.

David D Lewis and Jason Catlett. 1994. Heterogeneous uncertainty sampling for supervised learning. In *Machine learning proceedings 1994*, pages 148–156. Elsevier.

Bill Yuchen Lin, Dong-Ho Lee, Frank F. Xu, Ouyu Lan, and Xiang Ren. 2019. AlpacaTag: An active learning-based crowd annotation framework for sequence tagging. In *Proceedings of the 57th Annual Meeting of the Association for Computational Linguistics: System Demonstrations*, pages 58–63, Florence, Italy, July. Association for Computational Linguistics.

Xiaofei Lu. 2012. The relationship of lexical richness to the quality of esl learners' oral narratives. *The Modern Language Journal*, 96(2):190–208.

Simon Mille, Anja Belz, Bernd Bohnet, Emily Pitler, and Leo Wanner, editors. 2018. *Proceedings of the First Workshop on Multilingual Surface Realisation*, Melbourne, Australia, July. Association for Computational Linguistics.

Jekaterina Novikova, Oliver Lemon, and Verena Rieser. 2016. Crowd-sourcing nlg data: Pictures elicit better data. In *Proceedings of the 9th International Natural Language Generation conference*, pages 265–273.

Jekaterina Novikova, Ondřej Dušek, and Verena Rieser. 2017. The e2e dataset: New challenges for end-to-end generation. In *Proceedings of the 18th Annual SIGdial Meeting on Discourse and Dialogue*, pages 201–206.

Ehud Reiter. 2007. An architecture for data-to-text systems. In *Proceedings of the Eleventh European Workshop on Natural Language Generation*, pages 97–104. Association for Computational Linguistics.

Rico Sennrich, Barry Haddow, and Alexandra Birch. 2016. Neural machine translation of rare words with subword units. In *Proceedings of the 54th Annual Meeting of the Association for Computational Linguistics (Volume 1: Long Papers)*, pages 1715–1725.

Xiaoyu Shen, Ernie Chang, Hui Su, Jie Zhou, and Dietrich Klakow. 2020. Neural data-to-text generation via jointly learning the segmentation and correspondence. *arXiv preprint arXiv:2005.01096*.

Christopher Tosh and Sanjoy Dasgupta. 2018. Interactive structure learning with structural query-by-committee. In *Advances in Neural Information Processing Systems*, pages 1121–1131.

Ashish Vaswani, Noam Shazeer, Niki Parmar, Jakob Uszkoreit, Llion Jones, Aidan N Gomez, Łukasz Kaiser, and Illia Polosukhin. 2017. Attention is all you need. In *Advances in neural information processing systems*, pages 5998–6008.

Tsung-Hsien Wen, Milica Gašić, Nikola Mrkšić, Pei-Hao Su, David Vandyke, and Steve Young. 2015. Semantically conditioned LSTM-based natural language generation for spoken dialogue systems. In *Proceedings of the 2015 Conference on Empirical Methods in Natural Language Processing*, pages 1711–1721, Lisbon, Portugal, September. Association for Computational Linguistics.

Jason D. Williams, Eslam Kamal, Mokhtar Ashour, Hani Amr, Jessica Miller, and Geoff Zweig. 2015. Fast and easy language understanding for dialog systems with Microsoft language understanding intelligent service (LUIS). In *Proceedings of the 16th Annual Meeting of the Special Interest Group on Discourse and Dialogue*, pages 159–161, Prague, Czech Republic, September. Association for Computational Linguistics.

Jie Yang, Yue Zhang, Linwei Li, and Xingxuan Li. 2018. Yedda: A lightweight collaborative text span annotation tool. In *Proceedings of ACL 2018, System Demonstrations*, pages 31–36.

Demo Application for the AutoGOAL Framework

Suilan Estevez-Velarde[1], **Alejandro Piad-Morffis**[1], **Yoan Gutiérrez**[2,3],
Andrés Montoyo[2,3], **Rafael Muñoz**[2,3], and **Yudivián Almeida-Cruz**[1]

[1]School of Math and Computer Science, University of Havana, Cuba
{sestevez, apiad, yudy}@matcom.uh.cu
[2]University Institute for Computing Research (IUII), University of Alicante, Spain
[3]Department of Languages and Computing Systems, University of Alicante, Spain
{ygutierrez, montoyo, rafael}@dlsi.ua.es

Abstract

This paper introduces a web demo that showcases the main characteristics of the AutoGOAL framework. AutoGOAL is a framework in Python for automatically finding the best way to solve a given task. It has been designed mainly for automatic machine learning (AutoML) but it can be used in any scenario where several possible strategies are available to solve a given computational task. In contrast with alternative frameworks, AutoGOAL can be applied seamlessly to Natural Language Processing as well as structured classification problems. This paper presents an overview of the framework's design and experimental evaluation in several machine learning problems, including two recent NLP challenges. The accompanying software demo is available online[1] and full source code is provided under the MIT open-source license[2].

1 Introduction

The field of machine learning has applications across a wide range of computational problems in different domains. However, given the vast quantity of resources and technologies available, often one of the most difficult challenges is to select the best combination of them when a specific problem is faced. Researchers often spend a significant amount of time and computational resources exploring multiple approaches in search of optimal configurations. The field of automatic machine learning (AutoML) has risen to prominence as a principled alternative for finding optimal or close to optimal solutions to complex machine learning problems (Hutter et al., 2018). Several software libraries have been created, which leverage existing machine learning technologies and provide AutoML features built on them. Most existing AutoML tools focus on a specific family of algorithms (such as neural networks) or a specific problem setting (such as supervised learning from tabular data). Hence, despite the recent success of AutoML, several challenges still remain, specially in complex domains such as natural language processing, where tools and technologies from different sources must be combined.

This work presents AutoGOAL, a software library for AutoML that can seamlessly combine technologies and resources from different frameworks. To unify disparate APIs into a single interface, AutoGOAL proposes a novel graph-based representation for machine learning pipelines. Furthermore, a search strategy based on probabilistic grammatical evolution is used to discover optimal machine learning pipelines (Estevez-Velarde et al., 2019) whose components can be from different back-end libraries. A showcase web application is provided to illustrate the use of the framework.

The key features of AutoGOAL are:

Ease of use: AutoGOAL provides high-level classes that non-experts can use as black-box AutoML solutions, compatible with several data types including text, images and structured (tabular) data.

Multiple domains: AutoGOAL comes prepackaged with 133 plus adapters of existing algorithms, from 7 different back-end libraries, for multiple problems including text preprocessing, feature extraction,

---

[1]https://autogoal.github.io/demo
[2]https://autogoal.github.io

Proceedings of the 27th International Conference on Computational Linguistics, pages 18–22
Barcelona, Spain (Online), December 12, 2020.

dataset augmentation, dimensionality reduction, as well as supervised and unsupervised learning techniques.

Extensibility: AutoGOAL proposes a simple programming interface that developers can implement to create an automatically discoverable adapter for an existing technology from any machine learning framework.

This paper focuses on the engineering design of AutoGOAL by introducing a demo application using the library to solve several machine learning problems, organised as follow: Section 2 describes AutoGOAL from the perspective of a user of the library. Section 3 describes the library's design. Section 4 presents experimental results of the application of AutoGOAL to several different machine learning problems. Finally, Section 5 presents the conclusions and recommendations for future work.

2 Library Usage

AutoGOAL can be used as a software library in the Python programming language. This library is oriented towards two machine learning user profiles: non-experts and experts, and provides a High-Level and Low-Level API respectively.

High-Level API (non-experts): This API allows AutoGOAL to be used as a black-box classification or regression algorithm with an interface similar to the *scikit-learn* library (Pedregosa et al., 2011). Behind this interface, a complete process including preprocessing, feature selection, dimensionality reduction, and learning is performed. The user must define a dataset for training and evaluation, a metric to optimise (which defaults to *accuracy*) and the type of input and output data. In many cases AutoGOAL can automatically infer the input and output type from the dataset. Input and output types can vary from tabular data to complex types such as images, natural language text with different semantic structures, and combinations thereof. Figure 1 shows an illustrative example source code, specifically in the context of a text classification problem.

```
1  from autogoal.ml import AutoML
2  from autogoal.datasets import haha
3  # import lines for semantic datatypes
4
5  automl = AutoML(
6      # problem-specific input and output (semantic datatypes)
7      input=List(Sentences()),
8      output=CategoricalVector()
9      # additional parameters for timeout, memory, iterations, etc.
10 )
11
12 X, y = haha.load() # load problem-specific dataset
13 automl.fit(X, y)    # run optimisation
```

Figure 1: Example source code for running AutoGOAL on a specific dataset, in this case an NLP problem.

Low-Level API (experts): This API is designed for users with more experience that need control over the AutoML process. For this type of user, AutoGOAL provides a simple language for defining a grammar that describes the solution space. This is done using an object oriented approach were the user defines a Python class for each component of the solution (e.g., each algorithm) and annotates the parameters of these classes with attributes that describe the space of possible values, which can be primitive value types (i.e., numeric, string, etc.) and instances of other classes, recursively. Based on the annotations, AutoGOAL can automatically construct all possible ways in which the user classes can be instantiated. An example code of this process is available in the online documentation.[3]

---

[3]https://autogoal.github.io/examples/sklearn_simple_grammar/

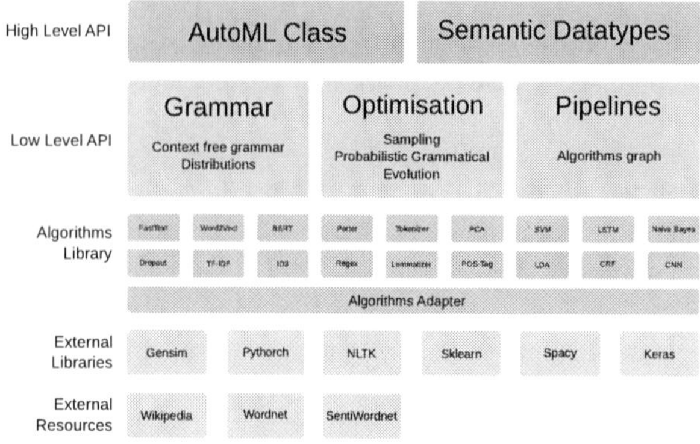

Figure 2: Overall architecture of the AutoGOAL framework.

3 Implementation Details

This section presents the overall architecture of the AutoGOAL library. For reference purposes, Figure 2 illustrates the most relevant components of AutoGOAL, ranging from the High-Level API down to the actual implementation of algorithm adapters and the interfaces to external resources and back-end libraries. The core of the AutoGOAL library is the Low-Level API, composed of the following elements (see Figure 2): a probabilistic context-free grammar module (*Grammar*); a sampling and optimisation module (*Optimisation*); and, a pipeline discovery module (*Pipelines*).

The *Grammar* module provides a set of type annotations that are used for defining the hyperparameter space of an arbitrary technique or algorithm. Each technique is represented as a Python class, and the corresponding hyperparameters are represented as annotated arguments of the `__init__` method, either primitive values (e.g., numeric, string, etc.) or instances of other classes, recursively annotated. Given a collection of annotated classes, this module automatically infers a context-free grammar that describes the space of all possible instances of those classes.

The *Optimisation* module provides sampling strategies that traverse a context-free grammar and recursively construct one specific instance following the annotations. Two optimisation strategies are implemented: random search and probabilistic grammatical evolution (O'Neill and Ryan, 2001). The latter performs a sampling/update cycle that selects the best performing instances according to some predefined metric (e.g., accuracy on a development set) and iteratively updates the internal probabilistic model of the sampler (Estévez-Velarde et al., 2020).

The *Pipelines* module provides an abstraction for algorithms to communicate with each other via an Facade pattern, i.e., the implementation of a method `run` with type-annotated input and output. Classes implementing this pattern are automatically connected in a graph of algorithms where each path represents a possible pipeline for solving a specific problem (defined by the input and output datatypes).

The High-Level API that provides the `AutoML` class (see Listing 1) and the *Semantic Datatypes* is built on top of this architecture, knitting together all the components of AutoGOAL. AutoGOAL also provides an Algorithms Library of pre-made adapters for existing machine learning technologies from External Libraries and Resources. A total of 133 algorithms from 7 different back-end libraries[4] are provided, several of which are semi-automatically created by code introspection (e.g., algorithms from *scikit-learn* and *nltk* which conform to a consistent API and the hyperparameters are documented in a consistent format), and the rest are manually added by the library developers. This library is undergoing continuous expansion. Additionally, a Docker image is provided with all optional dependencies and

---

[4]Including *scikit-learn*, *nltk*, *gensim*, *spacy*, *keras*, *pytorch*, among others.

back-end libraries already installed[5].

4 Evaluation

AutoGOAL has been evaluated in different domains and compared to other AutoML tools, including Auto-Weka (Thornton et al., 2013), TPOT (Olson and Moore, 2016), Auto-Sklearn (Feurer et al., 2015), and ML-Plan (Mohr et al., 2018), see Table 1. AutoGOAL is compared with other AutoML approaches in classic datasets (Dua and Graff, 2017) but can applied to more complex domains such as text classification in HAHA (Chiruzzo et al., 2019) and entity recognition in MEDDOCAN (Lara-Clares and Garcia-Serrano, 2019).

In terms of performance, AutoGOAL achieves comparative results with other AutoML tools in classic datasets, with similar computational cost (1 hour per run). However, AutoGOAL's main strength lies in its ability to combine different tools for solving complex problems beyond structured supervised learning, such as natural language processing, using virtually the same code, by specifying the input and output datatypes. In these domains AutoGOAL performs comparable to state-of-the-art solutions hand-crafted by human experts, while requiring considerably less expertise and effort (48 hours of execution).

Dataset	Cars	Credit G.	Abalone	Shuttle	Yeast	Dorothea	Gisette	HAHA	MEDD.
ML-Plan (Weka)	1.27	25.54	73.72	0.01	39.37	6.49	2.92	-	-
Auto-WEKA	0.66	26.50	73.46	0.12	39.72	-	3.90	-	-
ML-Plan (Sklearn)	0.34	24.56	73.77	0.02	39.52	8.69	2.76	-	-
Auto-Sklearn-v	1.38	25.95	82.92	0.02	40.51	6.32	2.56	-	-
Auto-Sklearn-we	1.26	25.39	80.59	0.02	38.99	6.02	2.24	-	-
TPOT	0.37	23.91	73.14	0.02	38.47	-	-	-	-
AutoGOAL	0.60	27.01	74.33	0.11	39.94	5.97	2.25	21.1	3.99

Table 1: Comparison of AutoGOAL and other AutoML systems for 9 classic machine learning datasets in terms of accuracy, except for MEDDOCAN, in which F_1 is used. Values for other systems were obtained from *ML-Plan* (Mohr et al., 2018).

5 Conclusion

In this paper we presented AutoGOAL, a new tool for AutoML that allows resources from different machine learning libraries to be combined and applied to different domains with little effort. AutoGOAL greatly simplifies the application of machine learning for non-expert users while providing powerful low-level components for experts to effectively optimise complex machine learning pipelines. The framework has been designed with extensibility as a priority, enabling the addition of new algorithms from any conceivable machine learning library by conforming to a simple interface. To demonstrate its usefulness, AutoGOAL is applied to different domains —including classic numeric datasets, text classification, and entity recognition— achieving competitive results with the state of the art. The software is provided freely for the research community along with a vast library of algorithms already implemented.

Acknowledgements

Funding: This research has been supported by a Carolina Foundation grant in agreement with University of Alicante and University of Havana. Moreover, it has also been partially funded by both aforementioned universities, the Generalitat Valenciana (*Conselleria d'Educació, Investigació, Cultura i Esport*) and the Spanish Government through the projects LIVING-LANG (RTI2018-094653-B-C22) and SIIA (PROMETEO/2018/089, PROMETEU/2018/089).

---

[5]https://hub.docker.com/repository/docker/autogoal/autogoal

References

Luis Chiruzzo, S Castro, Mathias Etcheverry, Diego Garat, Juan José Prada, and Aiala Rosá. 2019. Overview of haha at iberlef 2019: Humor analysis based on human annotation. In *Proceedings of the Iberian Languages Evaluation Forum (IberLEF 2019). CEUR Workshop Proceedings, CEUR-WS, Bilbao, Spain (9 2019)*.

Dheeru Dua and Casey Graff. 2017. UCI machine learning repository.

Suilan Estevez-Velarde, Yoan Gutiérrez, Andrés Montoyo, and Yudivián Almeida-Cruz. 2019. AutoML strategy based on grammatical evolution: A case study about knowledge discovery from text. In *Proceedings of the 57th Annual Meeting of the Association for Computational Linguistics*, pages 4356–4365, Florence, Italy, July. Association for Computational Linguistics.

Suilan Estévez-Velarde, Yoan Gutiérrez, Yudivián Almeida-Cruz, and Andrés Montoyo. 2020. General-purpose hierarchical optimisation of machine learning pipelines with grammatical evolution. *Information Sciences*, 543:58–71.

Matthias Feurer, Aaron Klein, Katharina Eggensperger, Jost Springenberg, Manuel Blum, and Frank Hutter. 2015. Efficient and robust automated machine learning. In *Advances in Neural Information Processing Systems*, pages 2962–2970.

Frank Hutter, Lars Kotthoff, and Joaquin Vanschoren, editors. 2018. *Automated Machine Learning: Methods, Systems, Challenges*. Springer. In press, available at http://automl.org/book.

Alicia Lara-Clares and Ana Garcia-Serrano. 2019. Key phrases annotation in medical documents: Meddocan 2019 anonymization task.

Felix Mohr, Marcel Wever, and Eyke Hüllermeier. 2018. ML-Plan: Automated machine learning via hierarchical planning. *Machine Learning*, 107(8):1495–1515, sep.

Randal S Olson and Jason H Moore. 2016. Tpot: A tree-based pipeline optimization tool for automating machine learning. In *Workshop on Automatic Machine Learning*, pages 66–74.

Michael O'Neill and Conor Ryan. 2001. Grammatical evolution. *IEEE Transactions on Evolutionary Computation*, 5(4):349–358.

F. Pedregosa, G. Varoquaux, A. Gramfort, V. Michel, B. Thirion, O. Grisel, M. Blondel, P. Prettenhofer, R. Weiss, V. Dubourg, J. Vanderplas, A. Passos, D. Cournapeau, M. Brucher, M. Perrot, and E. Duchesnay. 2011. Scikit-learn: Machine learning in Python. *Journal of Machine Learning Research*, 12:2825–2830.

Chris Thornton, Frank Hutter, Holger H Hoos, and Kevin Leyton-Brown. 2013. Auto-WEKA: Combined selection and hyperparameter optimization of classification algorithms. In *Proceedings of the 19th ACM SIGKDD international conference on Knowledge discovery and data mining*, pages 847–855. ACM.

Fast Word Predictor for On-Device Application

Huy Tien Nguyen[1,2,3]   Khoi Tuan Nguyen[1]   Anh Tuan Nguyen[1]   Thanh Lac Thi Tran[1]

[1] Zalo Research Center, Ho Chi Minh, Vietnam
[2] Faculty of Information Technology, University of Science, Ho Chi Minh city, Vietnam
[3] Vietnam National University, Ho Chi Minh city, Vietnam
{huynt,khoint3,anhnt7,thanhttl}@zalo.me

Abstract

Learning on large text corpora, deep neural networks achieve promising results in the next word prediction task. However, deploying these huge models on devices has to deal with constraints of low latency and a small binary size. To address these challenges, we propose a fast word predictor performing efficiently on mobile devices. Compared with a standard neural network which has a similar word prediction rate, the proposed model obtains 60% reduction in memory size and 100X faster inference time on a middle-end mobile device. The method is developed as a feature for a chat application which serves more than 100 million users.

1   Introduction

As a self-supervised learning task, next word prediction based on deep neural networks obtains robust performance by learning on large text corpora. Given a textual context as input, these models shown in Figure 1(a) encode the text to generate a probability distribution over a vocabulary for the next word. Although various neural networks have been developed for efficient computation and performance, the word embedding layer and softmax layer are still essential parts in these architectures. However, this approach faces a bottleneck for deploying on mobile devices that is the huge number of parameters in the word embedding matrix and softmax layer. For a vocabulary of N words and a word embedding of dimension D, the word embedding matrix takes $N \times D$ parameters and the softmax layer takes $H \times N$ where H is the dimension of encoded text. Yu (2018), for instance, proposed a recurrent neural network with $N = 15K$, and $D = H = 600$, so the word embedding matrix and softmax layer have 18M parameters in total. This cost has limited the applicability of deep neural networks on mobile devices for word prediction, word completion, and error correction tasks.

	Wikipedia	Social text
Vocabulary's size	1,364,714	897,846
Num of Bigrams	14,507,901	9,868,026
Avg num of accompanied words for one-grams	10.7	11
Avg num of accompanied words for bi-grams	5.1	4.9

Table 1: Statistics on 150 million tokens.

Various approaches have been proposed for deep neural compression. Matrix factorization (Nakkiran et al., 2015; Lu et al., 2016; Mehta et al., 2020) is applied to weight matrices to reduce model parameters while weight tying (Pappas et al., 2018; Pappas et al., 2018) shares the parameters of the embedding layer with those of the output classifier. In addition, network pruning and sharing are also efficient for reducing network complexity. For instance, Srinivas (2015) and Han (2015) explored the redundancy among neurons and propose to keep only the most the relevant parameters. Recently, Yu (2018) proposed an on-device word predictor employing shared matrix factorization and distillation to optimize memory

Proceedings of the 27th International Conference on Computational Linguistics, pages 23–27
Barcelona, Spain (Online), December 12, 2020.

and computation. These methods achieve promising results in memory reduction but limited efficiency in time constraint, especially on low-resource devices.

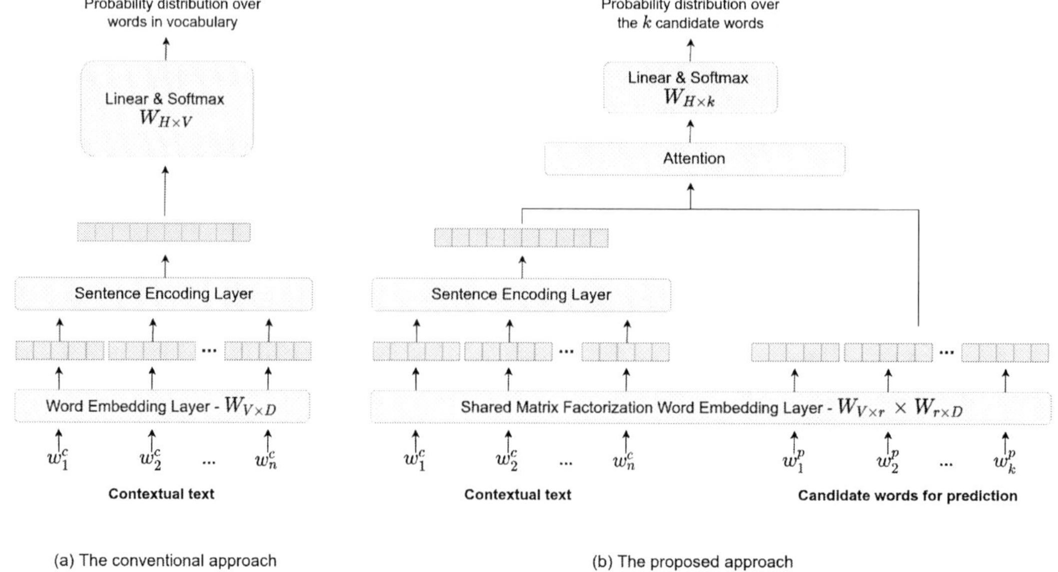

Figure 1: Approaches for word prediction

As we analysed the bottleneck, computation complexity primarily depends on vocabulary's size N, word embedding dimension D, and hidden dimension H related to the embedding matrix and softmax layer. Designed as a lookup table, the former have constant complexity, while the latter's operation is fully matrix multiplication. Therefore, our proposed approach is to reduce this softmax layer's computation. According to our analysis on 150 million tokens from Vietnamese Wikipedia text and social text listed in Table 1, the number of words frequently accompanied with each n-gram is quite small. This fact motivates us to design a model to consider candidate words for a given context instead of looking at all words in vocabulary for predicting the next word.

In this work, we propose an approach which takes a contextual text and list of candidate words as input, and output the probability distribution over these words via the attention mechanism (Vaswani et al., 2017). This architecture shown in Figure 1(b) decreases significantly the number of softmax layer's parameters and performs faster due to the attention operation's parallelization. In addition, our proposed model keeps the contextual words and potential words in the same embedding space which is recommended for learning language models (Press and Wolf, 2017). On middle-end devices (e.g., Samsung Galaxy A8 - 2016), the proposed model takes a smaller binary memory of 2.1MB (vs. 4.9MB) and faster inference time of 0.4ms (vs 41.2ms) while achieving a similar word prediction rate compared with a conventional neural model.

The next section describes in detail the model's architecture, how to obtain a list of candidate words for a given context, and the mechanism to construct training samples for efficiently learning and diminishing bias.

2 Proposed Method

2.1 N-gram potential words

Given a context, the way to obtain candidates for word prediction is a key factor to our model's performance. Through the statistics listed in Table 1, a tri-gram model is suitable for obtaining potential words. Experimental results shows that for a given bi-gram, next words belong to the top five accompanied words in 98% cases. Obviously, more grams (i.e., 4-grams, 5-grams) are employed, candidates are more fitted. However, storing these grams requires a bigger memory space which could exceed the conventional model's. For that reason, we choose the tri-gram model to query candidates for a given context. To optimize the tri-gram model's size, tri-grams with frequency less than a threshold T = 0.01% are filtered out; and candidates for these cases are randomly selected from the top frequent words in vocabulary. According to our evaluation, the difference in word prediction rate between the tri-gram model and the filtered one is minor.

2.2 Training samples

A straightforward approach of taking the n-gram potential words as candidates faces some drawbacks (i) bias in position since candidate lists are sorted by frequency; (ii) sensitive to uncommon words as the model learns local information (i.e., comparison between potential words) but lack of global information (i.e., comparison with other words). To address these challenges, some globally frequent words are added to the list of potential words to diversify comparison instead of only potential words. It also helps to avoid bias in the most frequent words. Then, the candidate lists are randomly permuted to remove position dependence in prediction. To enhance the ability of word comparison, negative samples, where the next word is not in the candidate list, are added.

2.3 Model architecture

Given a context $W^c = \{w_1^c, w_2^c, ..., w_n^c\}$ and candidate words $W^p = \{w_1^p, w_2^p, ..., w_k^p\}$, our model embeds each one-hot word $w_i \in \mathbb{R}^V$ into a low dimension vector $e_i \in \mathbb{R}^D$ via the shared matrix factorization (Yu et al., 2018) as follows:

$$e_i = w_i \times W_{V \times r} \times W_{r \times D} \tag{1}$$

Then, the context is encoded into a context embedding vector $e^C \in \mathbb{R}^D$ via a sentence embedding layer; and the attention $a \in \mathbb{R}^k$ (Vaswani et al., 2017) are computed between the query e^c and the keys e_i^p for generating a probability distribution $p(w_i^p|W^c)$ over the candidate words as follows:

$$e^c = Embed([e_1^c, e_2^c, ..., e_n^c]) \tag{2}$$
$$e^p = [e_1^p, e_2^p, ..., e_n^p] \tag{3}$$
$$a = Attention(e^c, e^p) \tag{4}$$
$$p = softmax(Wa + b) \tag{5}$$

where $W \in \mathbb{R}^{(k+1) \times k}$ and $b \in \mathbb{R}^{k+1}$ are a weight matrix and bias respectively. Instead of an output $p \in \mathbb{R}^k$, one slot is added to the output for negative sample prediction.

3 Experiment

According to the statistic shown in Table 1 and experimental results, we choose $k = 10$ including five words from the tri-gram model and five frequent words mentioned in Section 2.2. For the model's configuration, we empirically select $n = 15, r = 10, D = 100$ and a fully connected layer for embedding sentences. We collect 1.3B Vietnamese tokens for training and 130M Vietnamese tokens for evaluation from our social platform. We use top 50K frequent words as a vocabulary and replace out-of-vocabulary words with <UNK>. To improve the performance of models with matrix factorization, we employ the TA knowledge distillation (Mirzadeh et al., 2020) with $r = 50$ for the TA model. We use a Samsung Galaxy A8 version 2015 for evaluation.

3.1 Model evaluation

In Table 2, we report the comparison between the proposed approach and some baselines (i.e., N-gram, Tying weight (TW), and TW + Matrix factorization) in terms of inference speed per sample, model size and word prediction rate (WPR) which is a percentage of correct words prediction. Although compression methods help reduce model size, they show no improvement in computation time. Our Fast Prediction model achieves significant reduction for speed while remaining a competitive WPR. We observe that parameter reduction via matrix factorization hurts the conventional model's WPR (from 0.43

to 0.31). Our Fast Word Prediction, by contrast, lessens that effect via employing candidate words for narrowing learning space.

	WPR	Speed (ms)	Model Size
N-gram	0.36	0.05	1,5MB
Tying weight (Press and Wolf, 2017)	0.43	41.16	4,9MB
Tying weight + Matrix Factorization (Yu et al., 2018)	0.31	39.68	0.6MB
Fast Word Prediction	0.44	0.36	4.9MB* + 1.5MB^{+}
Fast Word Prediction + Matrix Factorization	0.41	0.4	0.6MB* + 1.5MB^{+}

Table 2: Performance comparison of our models and baselines. (*), and ($^{+}$) denote the size of neural networks and N-gram models respectively.

3.2 Candidate words evaluation

In this section, we evaluate various ways to construct a list of candidate words for a given context as follows:

- **Potential** (P): top 5 words from the tri-gram model. For context being out of the tri-gram model, the potential words are selected randomly from the vocabulary.

- **Potential + Random** (PR): add more 5 words randomly selected from the vocabulary.

- **Potential + Frequent** (PF): add more 5 words randomly selected from the top frequent words.

	P	PF
Potential	0.39	0.38
Potential + Random	0.4	0.39
Potential + Frequent	0.42	0.44

Table 3: Word Prediction Rate of three ways to obtain candidate words.

We evaluate these approaches on two validation sets: (i) samples constructed by P; (ii) samples constructed by PF. The experimental results in Table 3 support the claim mentioned in Section 1 that the approach PF prevents models from being biased towards frequent words compared with P and PR.

4 Conclusion

We have proposed an efficient approach for on-device word prediction. By making use of candidate words, TA distillation and matrix factorization, the model requires less parameters and computation while achieving a competitive performance. The model takes 2.1MB in memory and outputs a result in 0.4ms on the middle-end device. To optimize the model and keep it from being bias, we build a list of candidate words including potential words and frequent words. This approach of using candidate words is promising for enhancing user experience via personalizing the candidate list.

References

Song Han, Jeff Pool, John Tran, and William Dally. 2015. Learning both weights and connections for efficient neural network. In *Advances in neural information processing systems*, pages 1135–1143.

Zhiyun Lu, Vikas Sindhwani, and Tara N Sainath. 2016. Learning compact recurrent neural networks. In *2016 IEEE International Conference on Acoustics, Speech and Signal Processing (ICASSP)*, pages 5960–5964. IEEE.

Sachin Mehta, Rik Koncel-Kedziorski, Mohammad Rastegari, and Hannaneh Hajishirzi. 2020. Define: Deep factorized input token embeddings for neural sequence modeling. In *International Conference on Learning Representations*.

Seyed Iman Mirzadeh, Mehrdad Farajtabar, Ang Li, Nir Levine, Akihiro Matsukawa, and Hassan Ghasemzadeh. 2020. Improved knowledge distillation via teacher assistant: Bridging the gap between student and teacher. In *Proceedings of The Association for the Advancement of Artificial Intelligence*.

Preetum Nakkiran, Raziel Alvarez, Rohit Prabhavalkar, and Carolina Parada. 2015. Compressing deep neural networks using a rank-constrained topology. In *Proceedings of Annual Conference of the International Speech Communication Association (Interspeech)*, pages 1473–1477.

Nikolaos Pappas, Lesly Miculicich, and James Henderson. 2018. Beyond weight tying: Learning joint input-output embeddings for neural machine translation. In *Proceedings of the Third Conference on Machine Translation: Research Papers*, pages 73–83, Belgium, Brussels, October. Association for Computational Linguistics.

Ofir Press and Lior Wolf. 2017. Using the output embedding to improve language models. In *Proceedings of the 15th Conference of the European Chapter of the Association for Computational Linguistics: Volume 2, Short Papers*, pages 157–163, Valencia, Spain, April. Association for Computational Linguistics.

Suraj Srinivas and R. Venkatesh Babu. 2015. Data-free parameter pruning for deep neural networks. In Mark W. Jones Xianghua Xie and Gary K. L. Tam, editors, *Proceedings of the British Machine Vision Conference (BMVC)*, pages 31.1–31.12. BMVA Press, September.

Ashish Vaswani, Noam Shazeer, Niki Parmar, Jakob Uszkoreit, Llion Jones, Aidan N Gomez, Lukasz Kaiser, and Illia Polosukhin. 2017. Attention is all you need. In I. Guyon, U. V. Luxburg, S. Bengio, H. Wallach, R. Fergus, S. Vishwanathan, and R. Garnett, editors, *Advances in Neural Information Processing Systems 30*, pages 5998–6008. Curran Associates, Inc.

Seunghak Yu, Nilesh Kulkarni, Haejun Lee, and Jihie Kim. 2018. On-device neural language model based word prediction. In *Proceedings of the 27th International Conference on Computational Linguistics: System Demonstrations*, pages 128–131, Santa Fe, New Mexico, August. Association for Computational Linguistics.

Semantic search with domain-specific word-embedding and production monitoring in Fintech

Mojtaba Farmanbar, Nikki van Ommeren, Boyang Zhao
ING
Amsterdam, The Netherlands
{mojtaba.farmanbar, nikki.van.ommeren, boyang.zhao}@ing.com

Abstract

We present an end-to-end information retrieval system with domain-specific custom language models for accurate search terms expansion. The text mining pipeline tackles several challenges faced in an industry-setting, including multi-lingual jargon-rich unstructured text and privacy compliance. Combined with a novel statistical approach for word embedding evaluations, the models can be monitored in a production setting. Our approach is used in the real world in risk management in the financial sector and has wide applicability to other domains.

1 Introduction

Many industry-grade search engines exist (e.g. Elasticsearch) as general-purpose systems. While they have a general understanding of languages and includes search algorithms for document retrieval, their accuracy can be sub-optimal. This accuracy ultimately depends on domain specificity and the terms provided by the users.

This issue is particularly apparent in domains such as risk management. A critical function of the risk officers is knowing the relevant set of search terms to retrieve documents related to a specific topic. However, constructing a search criteria with all the appropriate search terms/phrases and their logical relations in the search engine remains complex, and can be prune to false-negatives and false-positives. While entity set expansion systems exist (among the earliest includes Google Sets), they are mostly using general-purpose language models (Zhang et al., 2020; Mamou et al., 2018) and thus not domain-specific.

In addition, building such an industry-grade domain-specific semantic search engine is challenging as this involves several additional considerations beyond simply an accurate language model. This includes: 1) extensive use of jargons, abbreviations, and unstructured data, 2) multiple languages relating to the same topic, 3) privacy compliance, and 4) performance monitoring of models on production.

In this paper, we describe an end-to-end information retrieval (IR) system with custom embeddings to address the aforementioned challenges. The system utilizes multiple advancements in Natural Language Processing (NLP) to process anonymized banking data. Capitalizing on our custom language models (in multiple languages and with multiple n-grams), we enable the automatic suggestion of highly relevant similar keywords, to ease the burden of requiring the user to build complex search queries. Additional pre-trained contextual embeddings are utilized for ranking by relevance. Lastly, we develop novel statistical methodologies for monitoring the stability of our language models on production.

2 Approach

We develop an end-to-end IR system, as depicted in Figure 1. The system, implemented in python, consists of 1) a text mining pipeline that preprocesses the records for indexing and for building language models, and 2) a front-end where the user queries the database with one or more search terms. The search terms are processed the same way by the text mining pipeline as for the records, and are further expanded to include similar words based on the trained domain-specific language models. The similar

Proceedings of the 27th International Conference on Computational Linguistics, pages 28–33
Barcelona, Spain (Online), December 12, 2020.

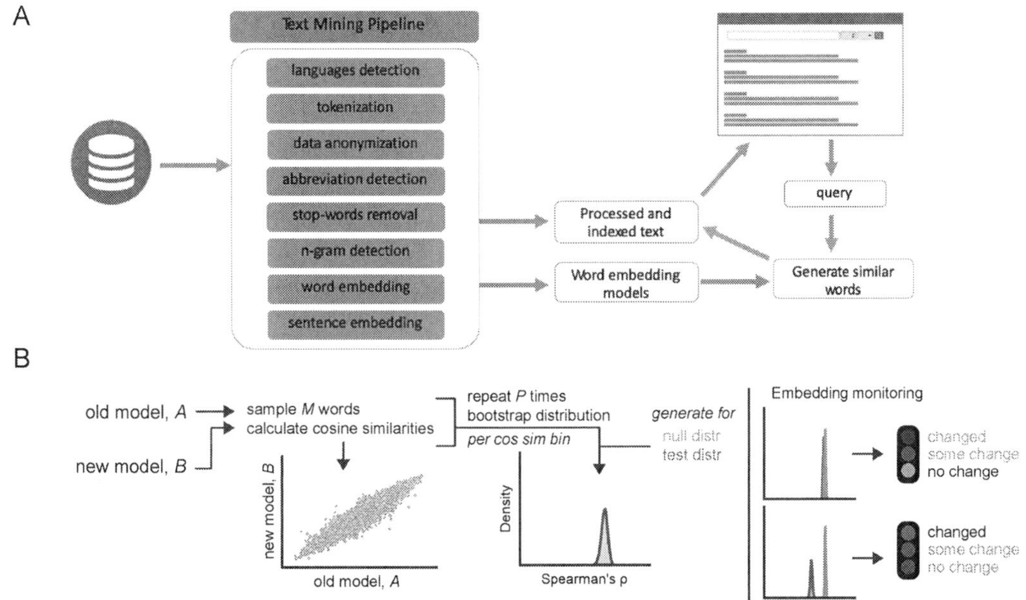

Figure 1: (A) IR system overview. Orange arrows indicate the preprocessing steps. Grey arrows indicate processing during real-time user queries. (B) Statistical method for monitoring word embeddings.

word expansion is thus a corpus-based approach and is based on the premise that similar words are distributionally related in similar contexts (known as the distributional hypothesis (Harris, 1954)).

2.1 Text mining pipeline

The text mining pipeline consists of several key components (Figure 1A). First, we integrate records from different data sources and unify them. As the records can be in different languages, we automatically detect languages based on specific patterns and with *spaCy*[1] so the appropriate language models can be used. Sensitive and identifiable information (e.g. names, phone numbers, employee identification numbers, etc) is retrieved and removed from the records. Abbreviations are extracted using the Shwartz-Hearst method (Schwartz and Hearst, 2003). The text is then cleaned using a combination of custom regular expressions and removal of stop-words and punctuations. We derive *n*-grams using *Gensim*[2] based on a PMI-like scoring method (Mikolov et al., 2013b). From the processed data, uni-, bi-, and tri-grams are jointly trained in deriving our custom word embeddings. Previous work suggests that multi-gram can improve on the quality of the obtained word embeddings (Gupta et al., 2019). In addition to word embeddings, we also derive document embeddings based on the cleaned text using pre-trained contextual multilingual universal sentence encoders. The embeddings are indexed for later ranking by relevance of the returning documents using FAISS (Johnson et al., 2017). The outputs of this pipeline is structured/processed data (along with the indexed version) and the trained word embeddings, which are used by our search engine in the front-end for query expansions.

2.2 Word embedding monitoring on production

We intend to monitor the stability of the word embeddings on production (Figure 1B). We capitalize on the intrinsic variability of the model from run to run (on the same data) to estimate its background variability. We can then determine if the extra variability between an old vs new model is different in comparison to this background variability. More specifically, for two given embeddings *A* and *B*, we first sample *M* words common to both embeddings. We derive *M-1* cosine similarity values (e.g. between

---

[1] https://spacy.io/
[2] https://radimrehurek.com/gensim/

Pre-trained general-purpose		Custom domain-specific
Word2Vec (GoogleNews)	GloVe (Wikipedia)	Word2Vec (domain-specific)
(confidentiality, 0.65)	(policy, 0.62)	(confidentiality, 0.82)
(security, 0.61)	(confidentiality, 0.56)	(datum_protection, 0.81)
(secrecy, 0.60)	(disclaimer, 0.54)	(disclosure, 0.73)
(anonymity, 0.59)	(policies, 0.51)	(banking_secrecy, 0.72)
(rights, 0.59)	(security, 0.49)	(bank_secrecy, 0.69)
(protection, 0.58)	(rights, 0.47)	(confidential_information, 0.64)
(oversight, 0.57)	(disclosure, 0.47)	(confidential, 0.63)
(identity, 0.57)	(reserved, 0.46)	(personal_datum, 0.63)

Table 1: Pre-trained and custom language models with similar terms retrieved for the word *privacy*. Cosine similarity values are shown in parentheses.

1st and 2nd word, 2nd and 3rd word, etc) based on A and again on B. We calculate the Spearman's correlation (ρ) of the cosine similarity values between A and B, binned based on A into 10 bins (from -1 to 1). This procedure is repeated P times to generate a bootstrapped distribution of ρ values (per bin). A Gaussian kernel density estimation is then fitted to each distribution. We perform this bootstrapping method on several pairs of embeddings. For embeddings generated from different runs on the same data, the resulting distribution constitutes the null distribution. For embeddings generated from old and new input data (during monitoring), the resulting distribution constitutes the test distribution. Comparison between the two distributions, as assessed by Jensen-Shannon divergence or Kolmogorov-Smirnov test statistic and with pre-defined thresholds enable monitoring of any substantial changes to the embeddings.

3 Experiments

We collect around 160K records in the financial sector. To compare across the different word embeddings, we use both pre-trained and custom-trained models. Pre-trained models have been previously trained on a large corpus such as the Wikipedia, Common Crawl, or Google News. Popular models include ones based on Word2Vec (Mikolov et al., 2013a) or GloVe (Pennington et al., 2014). While using these general-purpose language models saves training time and the need for custom preprocessing of data, they potentially lack domain-specific word semantics. Therefore, we also train custom Word2Vec Skip-gram word embeddings based on our datasets for English, French, and Dutch languages. We evaluate our models directly with the anonymized data as anonymization is required for compliance and regulatory reasons. For extrinsic word embedding evaluations, we build a gated recurrent unit (GRU)-based model with an embedding layer, followed by a 64-unit GRU, a 16-unit fully connected layer with ReLU activation, and an output layer with sigmoid activation. The model is trained with Adam optimizer and binary cross entropy loss function.

We also evaluate the quality of the information retrieval, viz. the precision achieved by relevance ranking based on the different sentence embedding models. Several models are examined, including TF-IDF, average of the Word2Vec (Google News), Word2Vec (domain-specific), or BERT (Devlin et al., 2019), CLS token of BERT, sentence BERT (sBERT) (Reimers and Gurevych, 2019), LASER (Artetxe and Schwenk, 2019), and different versions of universal sentence encoders (USE) (Cer et al., 2018) and multilingual universal sentence encoders (MUSE) (Yang et al., 2020). With the exception of TF-IDF and domain-specific Word2Vec, the other models are all taken as pre-trained models.

4 Results

4.1 Word embedding evaluations

We first want to evaluate if our custom domain-specific language models embed different word semantics compared to the pre-trained general-purpose models. When we examine for example the word *privacy*,

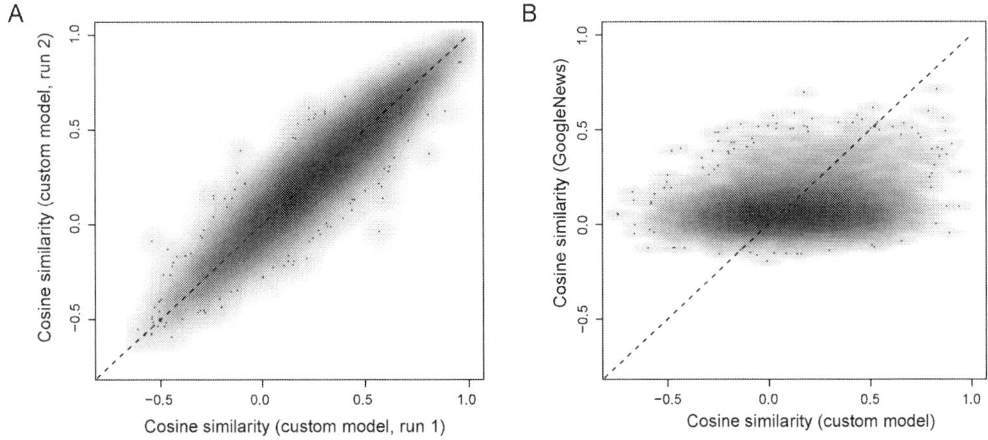

Figure 2: Sampling of 15,000 words from different embeddings, to show that the custom models retrieve relations that are vastly different from that compared to GoogleNews word relations.

we observe that GoogleNews- and Wikipedia-based embeddings associate *privacy* with many words that tend to have different semantics (Table 1). However, the custom word embeddings noticeably give a more consistent set of similar words and with higher similarity scores. Furthermore, the similar terms retrieved contain word phrases (bigrams) instead of just unigrams, and in many cases contain the word *bank*. As *privacy* is much more prevalent as a topic in our dataset related to the banking sector, these observations support a more relevant retrieval of similar words.

To assess whether the word relations are globally different between these models, we sample a large number of word pairs common in both custom and GoogleNews Word2Vec models, and evaluate their cosine similarity values based on either models. While we observe that the custom models from run to run maintain high concordance among the word relations (Figure 2A), they are vastly different from those based on GoogleNews models (Figure 2B).

In addition to our custom word embeddings encoding domain-specific word relations, we want to ensure they are good language models for other tasks. We perform extrinsic evaluations on the embeddings by building classifiers to assess whether the most common risk types can be predicted. Based on GRU-based neural network models, we observe that our custom embedding perform just as well as the much larger time-intensive pre-trained Google-News embedding (weighted F1 scores of 0.8 and 0.78, respectively). Therefore, our custom embedding encode language semantics on-par with pre-existing models, while retain domain-specificity for similar words extraction.

4.2 Word embedding monitoring

Our custom Word2Vec embeddings are rebuilt periodically with updated records to ensure the model is up-to-date and continues to capture the relevant vocabularies and semantics. For monitoring on production, we apply a statistical approach that measures the word relations and

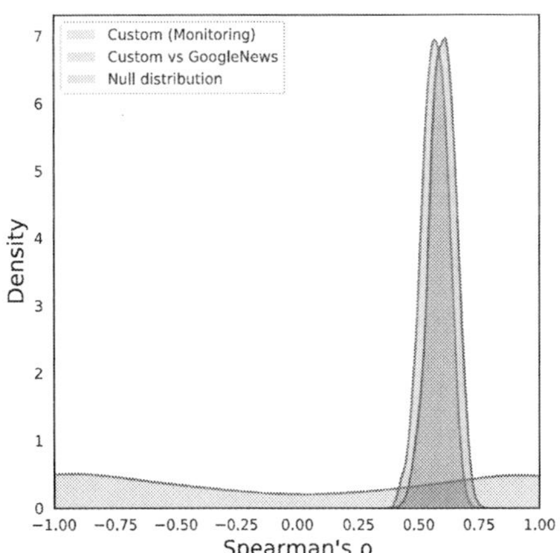

Figure 3: Monitoring word embeddings on production - illustrating that there are no substantial changes to the custom models being monitored.

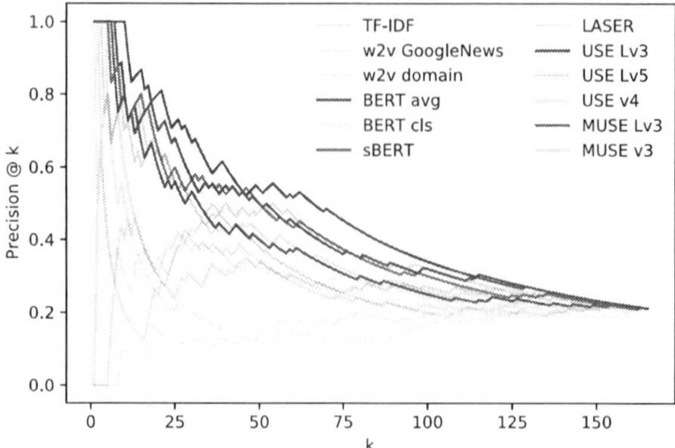

Model	Average precision
TF-IDF	0.29
Word2Vec (GoolgeNews)	0.29
Word2Vec (domain-specific)	0.33
BERT (average)	0.53
BERT (CLS)	0.18
sBERT	0.61
LASER	0.28
USE Lv3	0.75
USE Lv5	0.51
USE v4	0.44
MUSE Lv3	0.63
MUSE v3	0.58

Figure 4: Precision at k for the query *statistical model*, with selected models highlighted.

Table 2: Average precision for relevance ranking based on sentence embedding models for the query *statistical model*.

their distributional differences between a given and reference embeddings. We observe that the variations in the updated embeddings are not substantially different from the null distribution based on intrinsic stochasticity on the same dataset (Figure 3). When we compare to a substantially different word embedding (i.e. Word2Vec based on GoogleNews), we observe a dramatic change and shift in the distribution. Quantitatively, relative to the null distribution, we observe the updated custom Word2vec embeddings and GoogleNews Word2vec have Jensen-Shannon divergence of 0.22 and 0.70, respectively. We evaluate this for the embeddings of all different languages and n-grams, and set empirical thresholds for triggers on production.

4.3 Information retrieval evaluations

We assess the ranking quality of the returning documents across different sentence embedding models and queries. Using the query *statistical model* as example, we observe that the performance vastly differs (Figure 4 and Table 2). TF-IDF, average of word embeddings, and LASER models are unable to understand context, resulting in many highly ranked irrelevant documents that mention the word *model*, but in other contexts (e.g. business model, device model, car model, etc). CLS token of BERT is also found to be ineffective. BERT-based models are too slow for practical usage. Most strikingly, pre-trained universal sentence encoders (USE and MUSE) achieve higher precision, albeit variability in performance are observed among the various versions - likely due to difference in datasets and tasks used for training. We also finetune the USE/MUSE models for next sentence prediction, but no difference in performance is observed. These, among other examples, support the use of USE/MUSE for document embedding and relevance ranking in our system.

5   Conclusions

We present an end-to-end IR system used in production as a semantic search engine with intelligent keyword expansion and continual model monitoring. It addresses several challenges in handling multilingual domain-specific unstructured text and privacy compliance, and simplifying the derivation of keywords within a semantic class. Our experiments show that the custom word embeddings are distinct from general-purpose models, can present more relevant search terms, and can be monitored on production based on a novel statistical approach. We also show that different sentence embeddings differ vastly in performance and some, based on experimentation, can be used to improve relevance ranking. Overall our proposed solution is applicable for use in other domains.

Acknowledgements

We thank the anonymous reviewers for their feedback and colleagues at ING for helpful discussions.

References

Mikel Artetxe and Holger Schwenk. 2019. Massively multilingual sentence embeddings for zero-shot cross-lingual transfer and beyond. *Transactions of the Association for Computational Linguistics*, 7:597–610, mar.

Daniel Cer, Yinfei Yang, Sheng-yi Kong, Nan Hua, Nicole Limtiaco, Rhomni St. John, Noah Constant, Mario Guajardo-Cespedes, Steve Yuan, Chris Tar, Brian Strope, and Ray Kurzweil. 2018. Universal sentence encoder for English. In *Proceedings of the 2018 Conference on Empirical Methods in Natural Language Processing: System Demonstrations*, pages 169–174, Brussels, Belgium, November. Association for Computational Linguistics.

Jacob Devlin, Ming-Wei Chang, Kenton Lee, and Kristina Toutanova. 2019. BERT: Pre-training of deep bidirectional transformers for language understanding. In *Proceedings of the 2019 Conference of the North American Chapter of the Association for Computational Linguistics: Human Language Technologies, Volume 1 (Long and Short Papers)*, pages 4171–4186, Minneapolis, Minnesota, June. Association for Computational Linguistics.

Prakhar Gupta, Matteo Pagliardini, and Martin Jaggi. 2019. Better word embeddings by disentangling contextual n-gram information. In *Proceedings of the 2019 Conference of the North American Chapter of the Association for Computational Linguistics: Human Language Technologies, Volume 1 (Long and Short Papers)*, pages 933–939, Minneapolis, Minnesota, June. Association for Computational Linguistics.

Zellig S. Harris. 1954. Distributional structure. *Word*, 10(2-3):146–162.

Jeff Johnson, Matthijs Douze, and Hervé Jégou. 2017. Billion-scale similarity search with gpus. *arXiv preprint arXiv:1702.08734*.

Jonathan Mamou, Oren Pereg, Moshe Wasserblat, Ido Dagan, Yoav Goldberg, Alon Eirew, Yael Green, Shira Guskin, Peter Izsak, and Daniel Korat. 2018. Term set expansion based on multi-context term embeddings: an end-to-end workflow. In *Proceedings of the 27th International Conference on Computational Linguistics: System Demonstrations*.

Tomas Mikolov, Kai Chen, Greg Corrado, and Jeffrey Dean. 2013a. Efficient estimation of word representations in vector space. In *Proceedings of Workshop at ICLR*.

Tomas Mikolov, Ilya Sutskever, Kai Chen, Greg S Corrado, and Jeff Dean. 2013b. Distributed representations of words and phrases and their compositionality. In *Advances in neural information processing systems*, pages 3111–3119.

Jeffrey Pennington, Richard Socher, and Christopher Manning. 2014. GloVe: Global vectors for word representation. In *Proceedings of the 2014 Conference on Empirical Methods in Natural Language Processing (EMNLP)*, pages 1532–1543, Doha, Qatar, October. Association for Computational Linguistics.

Nils Reimers and Iryna Gurevych. 2019. Sentence-bert: Sentence embeddings using siamese bert-networks. In *Proceedings of the 2019 Conference on Empirical Methods in Natural Language Processing*. Association for Computational Linguistics, 11.

Ariel Schwartz and Marti Hearst. 2003. A simple algorithm for identifying abbreviation definitions in biomedical text. *Pacific Symposium on Biocomputing*, 4:451–62, 02.

Yinfei Yang, Daniel Cer, Amin Ahmad, Mandy Guo, Jax Law, Noah Constant, Gustavo Hernandez Abrego, Steve Yuan, Chris Tar, Yun-hsuan Sung, Brian Strope, and Ray Kurzweil. 2020. Multilingual universal sentence encoder for semantic retrieval. In *Proceedings of the 58th Annual Meeting of the Association for Computational Linguistics: System Demonstrations*, pages 87–94, Online, July. Association for Computational Linguistics.

Yunyi Zhang, Jiaming Shen, Jingbo Shang, and Jiawei Han. 2020. Empower entity set expansion via language model probing. In *Proceedings of the 58th Annual Meeting of the Association for Computational Linguistics*, pages 8151–8160.

CogniVal in Action: An Interface for Customizable Cognitive Word Embedding Evaluation

Anonymous COLING submission

Abstract

We demonstrate the functionalities of the new user interface for CogniVal. CogniVal is a framework for the cognitive evaluation of English word embeddings, which evaluates the quality of the embeddings based on their performance to predict human lexical representations from cognitive language processing signals from various sources. In this paper, we present an easy-to-use command line interface for CogniVal with multiple improvements over the original work, including the possibility to evaluate custom embeddings against custom cognitive data sources.

1 Introduction & Background

The system presented in this work is based on the CogniVal framework presented by Hollenstein et al. (2019). We present the first encompassing framework for cognitive word embedding evaluation. We improve and extend the original features of CogniVal and provide a simple command line interface for scalable and customized experiments. CogniVal is openly available at `https://github.com/ DS3Lab/cognival-cli` and can be easily installed with `pip`.

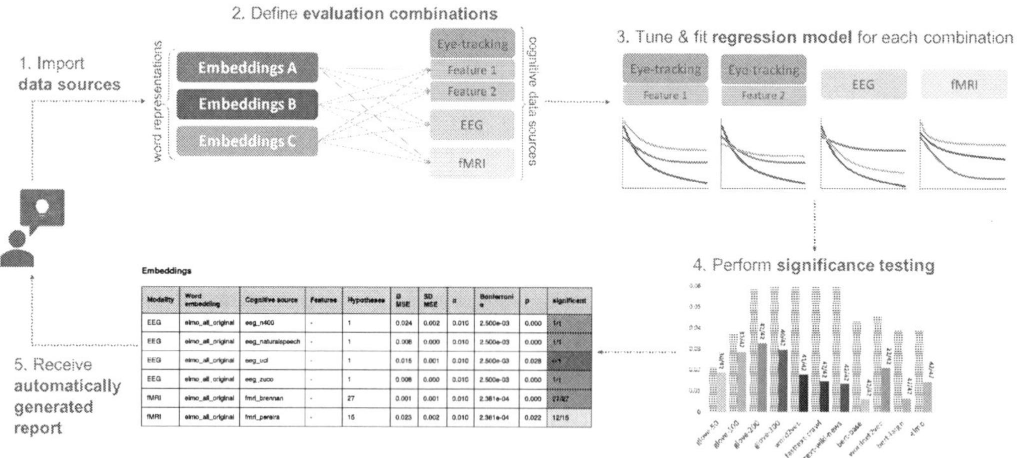

Figure 1: User interaction with the CogniVal interface.

Language models and word representations are the corner stones of state-of-the-art NLP models. Evaluating and comparing the quality of different word representations is a well-known, largely open challenge. While word representations and language models have proven very useful for NLP applications, their interpretability is inherently challenging. Interpretability is key for many NLP applications to be able to understand the algorithms' decisions. For a truly intrinsic evaluation of word embeddings more research about the cognitive plausibility of current language models is required (Rogers et al., 2018).

Proceedings of the 27th International Conference on Computational Linguistics, pages 34–40
Barcelona, Spain (Online), December 12, 2020.

Moreover, one of the challenges for computational linguistics is to build cognitively plausible models of language processing, i.e., models that integrate multiple aspects of human language processing at the syntactic and semantic level (Keller, 2010).

Currently, word embeddings are evaluated with extrinsic or intrinsic methods. Extrinsic evaluation is the process of assessing the quality of the embeddings based on their performance on downstream NLP tasks, e.g., sentiment analysis. However, embeddings can be trained and fine-tuned for specific tasks, but this does not mean that they accurately reflect the meaning of words. One the other hand, intrinsic evaluation methods, such as word similarity and word analogy tasks, merely test single linguistic aspects. These tasks are based on conscious human judgements, which can be biased by subjective factors (Nissim et al., 2019). It has been noted that current intrinsic evaluation methods do not capture the cognitive plausibility of the word embeddings and language models (Manning et al., 2020). Both intrinsic and extrinsic evaluation types often lack statistical significance testing and do not provide a global quality score. CogniVal addresses these issues and proposes an evaluation method based on cognitive lexical semantics.

Cognitive lexical semantics proposes that words are defined by how they are organized in the brain (Miller and Fellbaum, 1992). Recordings of brain activity play a central role in furthering our understanding of how human language works. Huth et al. (2016) showed in a neuroscientific study how words are represented in semantic maps across the brain. Moreover, language representations tuned on brain activity show improved performance on NLP tasks (Schwartz et al., 2019), and word representations trained on brain activity are more generalizable to unseen words (Fyshe et al., 2014). Hence, it seems natural to evaluate language models against human language processing data, as we have proposed with CogniVal (Hollenstein et al., 2019).

To accurately encode the semantics of words, we believe that embeddings, and full language models, should reflect this mental lexical representation. This allows us to evaluate word embeddings by quantifying their cognitive plausibility. There was a need for an extensive approach showing the utility of human cognitive data for language model evaluation and its correlation in predicting downstream task performance (Gladkova and Drozd, 2016). Evaluating word embeddings with cognitive language processing data has been proposed previously. For instance, Abnar et al. (2018) and Rodrigues et al. (2018) evaluated different embeddings by predicting the neuronal activity of nouns. Søgaard (2016) showed preliminary results in evaluating embeddings against continuous text stimuli in eye-tracking and functional magnetic resonance imaging (fMRI) data. Moreover, Beinborn et al. (2019) recently presented an extensive set of language–brain encoding experiments. Electroencephalography (EEG) data has been used for similar purposes. Schwartz and Mitchell (2019) and Ettinger et al. (2016) show that components of event-related potentials can successfully be predicted with neural network models and word embeddings. However, these approaches mostly focus on one modality of brain activity data from small individual cognitive datasets. The presence of only few and small data sources has been one reason why this type of evaluation has not been too popular until now (Bakarov, 2018).

Hence, for CogniVal we collected a wide range of cognitive data sources ranging from eye-tracking to EEG and fMRI to ensure coverage of a large vocabulary and of different features of the cognitive processes during language comprehension. The CogniVal command line interface (CLI) is the first tool to unify a diverse range of cognitive data sources of multiple recording modalities of cognitive processing signals and to provide a generic user interface. In this paper, we provide a user interface for CogniVal, which evaluates English word embeddings against the lexical representations of words in the human brain, recorded when passively understanding language. The CogniVal command line interface (CLI) makes large-scale cognitive word embedding evaluation accessible to NLP practitioners. It offers pre-processed cognitive data sources, readily provided for evaluation in a user-friendly interaction. It supports and complements other intrinsic and extrinsic evaluation methods for word embeddings. The CogniVal CLI is a unified framework, allowing the evaluation of a large set of existing pre-trained embeddings but also of custom word representations and language models on a large range of cognitive sources.

Interaction step	Example command(s)

1. Import data sources	```$ import cognitive-sources source=yourCustomSource```
	```$ import embeddings youCustomEmbeddings.zip```
	```$ import embeddings glove.6B.50```
	```$ import random-baselines glove.6B.50 num-baselines=10```

2. Define evaluation combinations	```$ config experiment cognitive-sources=[eeg_zuco] embeddings=[glove.6B.50]``` ```$ config experiment cognitive-sources=[eye-tracking_geco] embeddings=[fasttext]```
3. Fit regression models	```$ run embeddings=[glove.6B.50,glove.6B.100] cognitive-sources=[eye-tracking_geco] cognitive-features=[WORD_FIXATION_COUNT]```
4. Perform significance testing	```$ significance run_id=0 modalities=[eye-tracking, eeg, fmri] alpha=0.01 test=Wilcoxon```
5. Generate report	```$ report open-html=True```

Table 1: Main steps and example commands for using the CogniVal CLI for cognitive word embedding evaluation.

2 System Overview

The Cognival CLI is implemented in Python (version 3.7.4) and provides an interactive shell using `python-nubia`[1]. For the purpose of cognitive embedding evaluation, Hollenstein et al. (2019) collected and prepared 15 cognitive data sources and evaluated 6 pre-trained embedding types, including GloVe, word2vec, WordNet2Vec, FastText, ELMo and BERT. The command line interface provides these preprocessed data types. For details about the format of the cognitive data sources please refer to Hollenstein et al. (2019).

The evaluation process is automatized in the CogniVal CLI and works as as depicted in Figure 1. First, the user defines the general evaluation configuration, including path specifications and training parameters (command: `config`). If required, the user can then import custom word representations as well as custom cognitive data sources, using the `import` function. Second, the user specifies the embedding/cognitive-data combinations to be evaluated, as well as the hyper-parameter ranges for the neural regression models. Moreover, if requested, CogniVal generates random vectors of the same dimension of the embeddings to be evaluated. The embeddings can also be evaluated against this random baseline. As an improvement from Hollenstein et al. (2019), the CogniVal CLI automatically generates 10 sets of different random embeddings and averages over the results for a fairer comparison to a more robust baseline. The tuning (implemented through a grid search) and training of all models (n embeddings x m cognitive data sources) is fully automatized within the command `run`.

Thereafter, the user can either use the saved results as they are (i.e., mean squared errors for each word in the vocabulary), or they can run the significance testing (command: `significance`), which consists of a Wilcoxon signed-rank test for each hypothesis (i.e., for each embedding/cognitive-data evaluation combination), applying the Bonferroni correction for the multiple hypotheses problem, as described by Dror et al. (2018). Finally, the automatized generation of the report also includes significance testing by default and compares the results to the baseline of random embeddings before aggregating them. The dynamic HTML or PDF reports include all detailed results for the individual combinations, as well as aggregated over the modalities (see Figure 2). Table 1 presents the most important commands provided in the CogniVal CLI. Additionally, please refer to the GitHub repository for a full tutorial[2].

3 Use Cases

The target audience for the CogniVal CLI are NLP and machine learning practitioners and researchers developing word embeddings and in need of an evaluation benchmark. In this CogniVal demonstration paper, we describe the following two possible use case scenarios.

---

[1]`https://github.com/facebookincubator/python-nubia`
[2]`https://github.com/DS3Lab/cognival-cli/blob/master/cognival_tutorial.pdf`

Word embedding	Ø MSE Baseline	Ø MSE Proper	Significance
bert1	0.13905	0.00740	42/42
bert2	0.13974	0.00760	42/42
bert3	0.14057	0.00705	42/42
bert4	0.14013	0.00708	42/42
bert5	0.13949	0.00732	42/42
bert6	0.14030	0.00753	42/42
bert7	0.13835	0.00760	42/42
bert8	0.13772	0.00733	42/42
bert9	0.14116	0.00729	42/42
bert10	0.13918	0.00757	42/42
bert11	0.13794	0.00755	42/42
bert12	0.13936	0.00715	42/42

(a) Automatically generated result table.

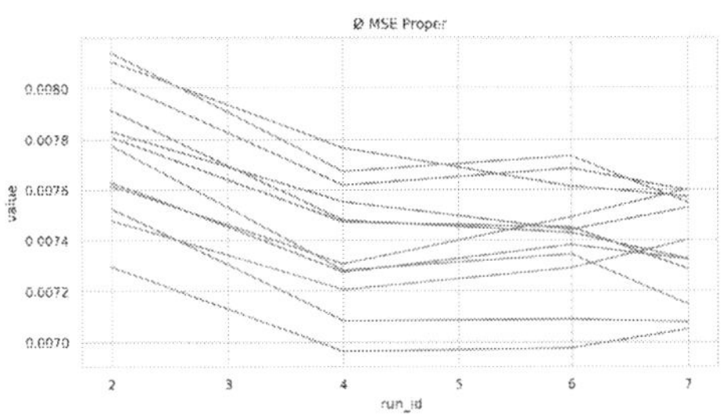

(b) Plot over time: When adding more eye-tracking features in each run, the aggregated results become more precise. Each colored line represents a different BERT layer.

Figure 2: Snippets from an automatically generated result report in the CogniVal CLI.

Scenario 1: Custom Word Embeddings & Cognitive Data Sources

One of the most relevant features of the CogniVal CLI is the possibility to upload custom word representations from any language model. Any type of word embedding can be imported into the system as text or binary files, and can then be evaluated against the available cognitive data sources and compared to the other embeddings included in CogniVal by default. Moreover, the automated versioning and reporting supports the development process of new embeddings by readily generating plots over the course of time to show whether the performance of the embeddings in development is improving or deteriorating across multiple runs.

In addition, custom cognitive data sources can also be imported into the CogniVal interface. This feature allows the user to add more cognitive language processing data as more of these datasets become available (Alday, 2019). Through these features CogniVal becomes a generic framework for cognitive word embedding evaluation and drastically increases the number of possible applications in any language.

Scenario 2: Complementary Benchmark & Evaluation Over Time

A second use case scenario for the CogniVal CLI is to use the cognitive word embedding evaluation as a complementary evaluation and a benchmark for embedding selection. If the user wants to compare the results achieved by their embeddings on CogniVal to other intrinsic or extrinsic results achieved with the same embeddings, the CLI allows to upload external results into the result directory and run the significance testing and aggregation report on all available results. Hence, CogniVal can easily be extended to include external results and can be leveraged as a tool for embedding selection. Furthermore, CogniVal can be used during the development of language models. If one is comparing a certain checkpoint of a language model to extrinsic results on a downstream task, the cognitive evaluation can help to ensure that the word representations are not overfitting on the downstream task and that they still maintain cognitive plausibility. To this end, the automatic report generated in the CogniVal CLI also includes plots to show changes over various runs, which can be very useful during the development of new language models or fine-tuning of existing pre-trained language models (see Figure 2b).

4   Example Application: Comparison of BERT Layers

As an exemplary use case scenario for the CogniVal CLI, we analyze the performance of different layers of BERT pre-trained contextual word representations on all available cognitive data sources of eye-

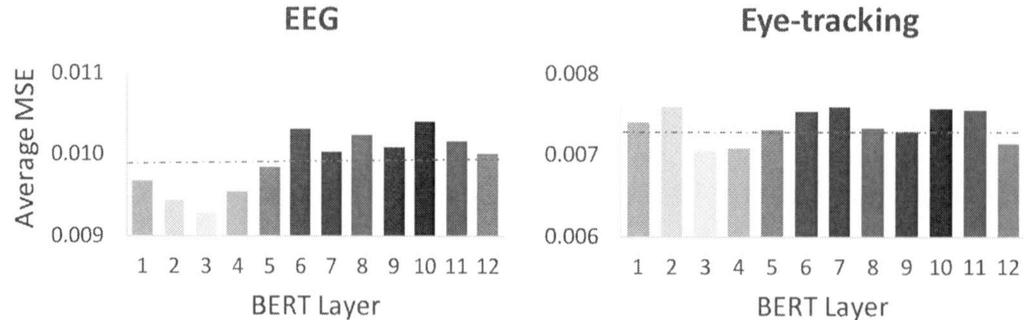

Figure 3: CogniVal results on evaluating the 12 layers of a BERT model against all available EEG and eye-tracking data sources.

tracking and EEG. Transformer-based language models such as BERT are widely used in state-of-the-art NLP, but their inner workings are still largely unknown (Rogers et al., 2020). We extract word-level BERT embeddings (Devlin et al., 2019) for all words where there is cognitive data available. Using the bert-as-service package[3] we extract the hidden states of all 12 layers of the BERT base uncased model with 768 dimensions. Subsequently, using the new CogniVal functionality to load custom embeddings, we import the BERT states of each layer easily into the CogniVal interface. We set the configuration to run all experiments against the 10-fold random baseline, with the following parameters for training: 3 fold cross-validation, a hidden layer of 200 dimensions, 20% validation split, batch size of 128, and ReLu activation functions.

The results of this example application are presented in Figure 3. In addition, Figure 2a shows the numerical summary of the results of BERT embeddings predicting eye-tracking features as it is presented in the automatically generated report, including the results of the random baselines and the results of the significance testing. While all hypotheses tested on the BERT layers proved to be statistically significant against the random baseline (4 EEG hypotheses – one for each dataset, and 42 eye-tracking hypotheses – one for each feature), there are visible differences in performance between the layers. Surprisingly, for both EEG and eye-tracking, layer 3 performs best. The results also show, how the last layer performs very closely to the average of all layers (dashed line). This finding reflects the original performance of the layers of the BERT base model on downstream NLP tasks (Devlin et al., 2019). It is also in line with Toneva and Wehbe (2019), who find that the lower layers perform best at predicting neural activation for short context ranges. Lin et al. (2019) show that the lower layers have the most linear word order information, which is likewise reflected in our results. This application scenario show how Cognival can be used to explore and support findings concerning the interpretability of language models.

5 Conclusion & Future Work

In this demonstration paper, we presented the new command line interface for CogniVal. The CogniVal CLI builds upon the work by Hollenstein et al. (2019) and extends it with various new features, especially the ability to evaluate custom embeddings against custom cognitive data sources. We described the functionalities of the tool as well as various use cases and an application scenario. The Cognivsl CLI aims at improving the accessibility and usability of cognitive embedding evaluation for NLP practitioners. CogniVal is still under active research and will be extended to additionally support the evaluation of sentence embeddings and further languages.

Acknowledgements

We thank Antonio de la Torre and Leonard von Kleist for their contributions to the command line interface.

---

[3]https://github.com/hanxiao/bert-as-service

References

Samira Abnar, Rasyan Ahmed, Max Mijnheer, and Willem Zuidema. 2018. Experiential, distributional and dependency-based word embeddings have complementary roles in decoding brain activity. In *Proceedings of the 8th Workshop on Cognitive Modeling and Computational Linguistics (CMCL 2018)*, pages 57–66.

Phillip M Alday. 2019. M/EEG analysis of naturalistic stories: A review from speech to language processing. *Language, Cognition and Neuroscience*, 34(4):457–473.

Amir Bakarov. 2018. Can eye movement data be used as ground truth for word embeddings evaluation? In *Proceedings of the Eleventh International Conference on Language Resources and Evaluation (LREC 2018)*.

Lisa Beinborn, Samira Abnar, and Rochelle Choenni. 2019. Robust evaluation of language-brain encoding experiments. *International Journal of Computational Linguistics and Applications*.

Jacob Devlin, Ming-Wei Chang, Kenton Lee, and Kristina Toutanova. 2019. BERT: Pre-training of deep bidirectional transformers for language understanding. In *Proceedings of the 2019 Conference of the North American Chapter of the Association for Computational Linguistics: Human Language Technologies, Volume 1 (Long and Short Papers)*, pages 4171–4186.

Rotem Dror, Gili Baumer, Segev Shlomov, and Roi Reichart. 2018. The hitchhiker's guide to testing statistical significance in natural language processing. In *Proceedings of the 56th Annual Meeting of the Association for Computational Linguistics (Volume 1: Long Papers)*, pages 1383–1392.

Allyson Ettinger, Naomi Feldman, Philip Resnik, and Colin Phillips. 2016. Modeling N400 amplitude using vector space models of word representation. In *CogSci*.

Alona Fyshe, Partha P Talukdar, Brian Murphy, and Tom M Mitchell. 2014. Interpretable semantic vectors from a joint model of brain-and text-based meaning. In *Proceedings of the 52nd Annual Meeting of the Association for Computational Linguistics (Volume 1: Long Papers)*, pages 489–499.

Anna Gladkova and Aleksandr Drozd. 2016. Intrinsic evaluations of word embeddings: What can we do better? In *Proceedings of the 1st Workshop on Evaluating Vector-Space Representations for NLP*, pages 36–42.

Nora Hollenstein, Antonio de la Torre, Nicolas Langer, and Ce Zhang. 2019. CogniVal: A framework for cognitive word embedding evaluation. In *Proceedings of the 23nd Conference on Computational Natural Language Learning*.

Alexander G Huth, Wendy A de Heer, Thomas L Griffiths, Frédéric E Theunissen, and Jack L Gallant. 2016. Natural speech reveals the semantic maps that tile human cerebral cortex. *Nature*, 532(7600):453–458.

Frank Keller. 2010. Cognitively plausible models of human language processing. In *Proceedings of the 48th Annual Meeting of the Association for Computational Linguistics: Short Papers*, pages 60–67.

Yongjie Lin, Yi Chern Tan, and Robert Frank. 2019. Open Sesame: Getting inside BERT's linguistic knowledge. In *Proceedings of the 2019 ACL Workshop BlackboxNLP: Analyzing and Interpreting Neural Networks for NLP*, pages 241–253.

Christopher D Manning, Kevin Clark, John Hewitt, Urvashi Khandelwal, and Omer Levy. 2020. Emergent linguistic structure in artificial neural networks trained by self-supervision. *Proceedings of the National Academy of Sciences*.

George A Miller and Christiane Fellbaum. 1992. WordNet and the organization of lexical memory. In *Intelligent tutoring systems for foreign language learning*, pages 89–102. Springer.

Malvina Nissim, Rik van Noord, and Rob van der Goot. 2019. Fair is better than sensational: Man is to doctor as woman is to doctor. *arXiv preprint arXiv:1905.09866*.

Joao António Rodrigues, Ruben Branco, João Silva, Chakaveh Saedi, and António Branco. 2018. Predicting brain activation with WordNet embeddings. In *Proceedings of the Eight Workshop on Cognitive Aspects of Computational Language Learning and Processing*, pages 1–5.

Anna Rogers, Shashwath Hosur Ananthakrishna, and Anna Rumshisky. 2018. What's in your embedding, and how it predicts task performance. In *Proceedings of the 27th International Conference on Computational Linguistics*, pages 2690–2703.

Anna Rogers, Olga Kovaleva, and Anna Rumshisky. 2020. A primer in BERTology: What we know about how BERT works. *arXiv preprint arXiv:2002.12327*.

Dan Schwartz and Tom Mitchell. 2019. Understanding language-elicited EEG data by predicting it from a fine-tuned language model. In *Proceedings of the 2019 Conference of the North American Chapter of the Association for Computational Linguistics: Human Language Technologies, Volume 1 (Long and Short Papers)*, pages 43–57.

Dan Schwartz, Mariya Toneva, and Leila Wehbe. 2019. Inducing brain-relevant bias in natural language processing models. In *Advances in Neural Information Processing Systems*, pages 14100–14110.

Anders Søgaard. 2016. Evaluating word embeddings with fMRI and eye-tracking. In *Proceedings of the 1st Workshop on Evaluating Vector-Space Representations for NLP*, pages 116–121.

Mariya Toneva and Leila Wehbe. 2019. Interpreting and improving natural-language processing (in machines) with natural language-processing (in the brain). In *Advances in Neural Information Processing Systems*, pages 14928–14938.

A Multilingual Reading Comprehension System for more than 100 Languages

Anthony Ferritto[1*]   **Sara Rosenthal**[1*]   **Mihaela Bornea**[1]   **Kazi Hasan**[2]
Rishav Chakravarti[1]   **Salim Roukos**[1]   **Radu Florian**[1]   **Avirup Sil**[1†]

[1]IBM Research AI   [2]IBM Watson
aferritto@ibm.com,
{sjrosenthal, mabornea, kshasan, rchakravarti, roukos, raduf, avi}@us.ibm.com

Abstract

This paper presents M-GAAMA, a Multilingual Question Answering architecture and demo system. This is the first multilingual machine reading comprehension (MRC) demo which is able to answer questions in over 100 languages. M-GAAMA answers questions from a given passage in the same or a different language. It incorporates several existing multilingual models that can be used interchangeably in the demo such as M-BERT and XLM-R. The M-GAAMA demo also improves language accessibility by incorporating the IBM Watson machine translation widget to provide additional capabilities to the user to see an answer in their desired language. We also show how M-GAAMA can be used in downstream tasks by incorporating it into an END-TO-END-QA system using CFO (Chakravarti et al., 2019). We experiment with our system architecture on the Multi-Lingual Question Answering (MLQA) and the CORD-19 COVID (Wang et al., 2020; Tang et al., 2020) datasets to provide insights into the performance of the system.

1   Introduction

Recent advances in open domain question answering (QA) have mostly revolved around machine reading comprehension (MRC) (Rajpurkar et al., 2018; Yang et al., 2018). The MRC task is to read and comprehend a given text and then answer questions based on it. Our monolingual MRC approach (Pan et al., 2019) has the capability of being applied to train many Language Models (LMs) such as BERT (Devlin et al., 2019) and RoBERTa (Liu et al., 2019). We achieve the 2nd rank[1] on the Google Natural Questions (Kwiatkowski et al., 2019) leaderboard[2]. In this paper, we expand our approach by introducing new multilingual capabilities using models such as Multilingual-BERT (M-BERT) (Devlin et al., 2019) and XLM-R (Conneau et al., 2019). This addition has the capability of transcending language boundaries to *104* languages. Figure 1 shows examples of QA pairs from the MLQA dataset (Lewis et al., 2019). To the best of our knowledge, this is the first published demo of a Multi-Lingual QA system. We achieve this by introducing a novel multilingual component to our QA GAAMA (Go Ahead, Ask Me Anything) (Chakravarti et al., 2019) pipeline.

We introduce M-GAAMA, a new system that performs cross-lingual MRC where a given question and context can be in the same or different languages. The system extracts the answer from the context language. Then, the demo utilizes the SOTA IBM Watson machine translation widget to return the answer translated in the desired language of the user[3]. This breaks the language barrier for users who don't understand the given source text but want their question answered effectively and accurately.

In addition, we also show how M-GAAMA can be used in downstream tasks by incorporating it with CFO (Chakravarti et al., 2019), in an end-to-end QA system and demo. We show that this can be extended to perform multilingual QA by utilizing a language identifier to first gather the (target) language in which

---

* Equal Contribution

† Corresponding author.

This work is licensed under a Creative Commons Attribution 4.0 International License. License details: http://creativecommons.org/licenses/by/4.0/.

[1]At the time of writing of this paper.

[2]https://ai.google.com/research/NaturalQuestions/leaderboard

[3]Currently available in 36 languages.

Proceedings of the 27th International Conference on Computational Linguistics, pages 41–47
Barcelona, Spain (Online), December 12, 2020.

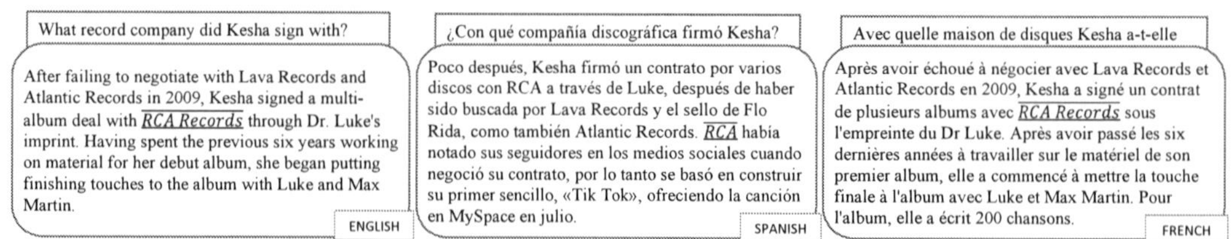

Figure 1: Examples of Q/C pairs about Kesha in three languages that our system answers correctly: English, Spanish, and French. The first two examples originate from the MLQA challenge. The answers are shown as $\overline{answer}$.

the question was asked. END-TO-END-QA then retrieves passages from an index in the appropriate target language and runs our multilingual MRC system on it. Since the answer is extracted from the target language, no translation is required.

We first demonstrate the effectiveness of M-GAAMA on the MLQA dataset and then also show its effectiveness on the CORD-19 (Wang et al., 2020; Tang et al., 2020) corpus which contains research articles regarding COVID-19. The COVID-19 pandemic has caused an abundance of research to be published on a daily basis. Not all of the articles are available in English, and people want to ask questions in their native language. Providing the capability to ask questions on research in all languages is vital for ensuring that important and recent information is not overlooked and available to everyone. We show that M-GAAMA has the capability of providing this information for all language speakers and articles by finding answers in translated CORD-19 articles.

In summary, our contribution is the first published multi-lingual QA demo which works in over 100 languages. It returns an appropriate answer in the language that the question was originally asked. It incorporates several multilingual components including multilingual LMs, machine translation, and indexed corpora in multiple languages.

The rest of the paper is organized as follows: We first discuss related work, then talk about the data used in our experiments and models. Sections 4 and 5 discuss the demo system and model architecture. Finally, we discuss the Model and Runtime Experiments on MLQA (Lewis et al., 2019) and the COVID-19 CORD-19 dataset (Wang et al., 2020; Tang et al., 2020) in Section 6.

2 Related Work

Few other QA demos exist; BERTSerini (Yang et al., 2019), leverages the Anserini IR toolkit (Yang et al., 2017) to extract relevant documents given a question, then uses BERT-based techniques (Devlin et al., 2019) to extract the correct answer. However, their demo is designed to perform only mono-lingual English QA. The GAAMA and CFO (Chakravarti et al., 2019) demos also only performs English QA. In contrast, M-GAAMA and our downstream END-TO-END-QA task perform cross-lingual QA.

Several cross lingual large scale representations have been created by training a large scale transformer (Vaswani et al., 2017) based masked language model on text in multiple languages. The use of pretrained multilingual language models such as M-BERT (Devlin et al., 2019), XLM (Lample and Conneau, 2019), and XLM-R (Conneau et al., 2019) achieve the previous SOTA on cross-lingual tasks including question answering (Lewis et al., 2019) (Conneau et al., 2019). We train our underlying MRC system with these pre-trained language models and achieve results that are consistently as strong as prior work.

Many datasets for English MRC have been introduced with annotated Wikipedia documents including (Rajpurkar et al., 2016; Rajpurkar et al., 2018; Yang et al., 2018; Kwiatkowski et al., 2019). Fewer resources are available for the cross-lingual setting. The MLQA (Lewis et al., 2019) dataset contains parallel instances in 7 languages where the context is found in Wikipedia. The TyDiQA (Clark et al., 2020) dataset containes instances in 11 languages. However, TyDiQA is not parallel and it only has instances where the question and context are in the same language.

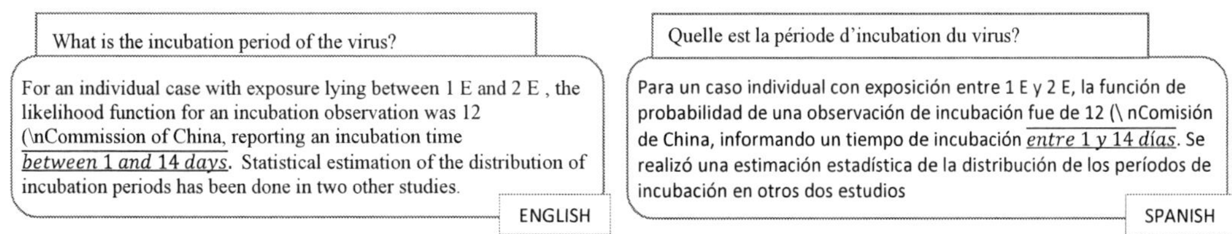

Figure 2: Examples of Q/C pairs about COVID-19. The answers are shown as $\overline{answer}$.

3 Data

We test the multilingual capabilities incorporated into our QA system by running experiments on the MLQA dataset (Lewis et al., 2019). The dataset consists of seven languages: English (en), Spanish (es), German (de), Arabic (ar), Hindi (hi), Vietnamese (vi), and Chinese (zh). To achieve a multilingual parallel QA benchmark the authors apply a novel alignment strategy on Wikipedia articles by identifying Wikipedia sentences with the same meaning in multiple languages. Passages containing these sentences are then presented to the annotators who write questions that are now answerable in multiple languages. We consider this a good resource for evaluating multilingual capabilities on different pairs of languages (e.g., context (c) in English, question (q) in German) due to the parallel q/c pairs available in the corpus. In addition, we use SQUAD 1.1 (Rajpurkar et al., 2016), which is significantly larger, but only contains English data, for training in a zero-shot scenario.

We also explore QA on COVID-19 articles in a zero-shot scenario to show the relevance and importance of multilingual QA in current events. CovidQA 0.1 (Wang et al., 2020) contains 124 question and document pairs. The dataset comprises of (question, scientific article, exact answer) triples that have been manually created from the literature review page of Kaggles COVID-19 Open Research Dataset Challenge (Tang et al., 2020). They manually identified the exact answer span as a verbatim extract from the document. We converted their data into SQUAD format for our experiments. We create a multilingual COVID-19 QA dataset using machine translation. We translate both the questions and context in Spanish and Chinese. We align the gold answer between the English and the translated dataset by marking the gold answer with pseudo-HTML tags prior to translation. We recovered the translated answers for all questions. An example of a QA pair in English and Spanish is shown in Figure 2.

4 Demo

In this section we describe the interface for our M-GAAMA demo. We then show an END-TO-END-QA demo as an example that builds upon M-GAAMA using prior work (Chakravarti et al., 2019).

M-GAAMA is a gRPC (Talvar, 2016) server which wraps our LMs for MRC. M-GAAMA provides an MRC interface which can answer questions in over 100 languages. We use M-BERT and XLM-R LMs to drive M-GAAMA's multilingual support. In addition, we provide a Language Translation component made available as a Javascript widget[4] to allow the user to see the answer in the question language or any other language of choice. The M-GAAMA interface weaves the components together using the ReactJS framework[5]. Providing M-GAAMA as a gRPC server allows it to be quite flexible. This enables it to seamlessly transition between being a standalone system and integrating with larger systems. We show this via the downstream END-TO-END-QA task described below.

END-TO-END-QA builds upon M-GAAMA, with a full IR-MRC pipeline. Information Retrieval is obtained using an Elasticsearch index[6] for each language[7]. The user can ask a question in any language for which an index exists. The language of the question is identified using the 'langid' toolkit (Lui and Baldwin, 2012) to determine the appropriate index. The appropriate index is then searched for documents in the target language. These documents are then evaluated together with the user's question

---

[4] https://www.ibm.com/watson/services/language-translator/

[5] https://reactjs.org/

[6] https://hub.docker.com/_/elasticsearch/

[7] In our implementation we built an index in English and Spanish as a proof of concept.

F1	MLQA									COVID-19		
	en	es	de	ar	hi	vi	zh	XLT	G-XLT	en	es	zh
ROBERTA$_L$	84.4	-	-	-	-	-	-	-	-	27.1	-	-
M-BERT	80.4	66.7	61.3	51.9	50.7	61.6	60.2	61.8	52.1	22.3	17.0	20.5
XLM-R$_B$	80.1	67.6	63.0	56.3	61.1	66.2	61.6	65.1	41.2	21.9	19.0	17.0
XLM-R$_L$	**83.9**	**74.0**	**69.9**	**66.3**	**71.2**	**74.0**	**69.9**	**72.7**	**67.9**	**27.0**	**28.7**	**25.0**

Table 1: (Left) F1 score on the MLQA test set for the cross-lingual transfer task (XLT) per language and the mean XLT and G-XLT scores. Training data is SQUAD 1.1. B is the Base model and L is the Large model. (Right) F1 XLT scores on the CORD-19 dataset when training on SQUAD 1.1 in three languages.

by M-GAAMA. Finally, answer spans are de-duplicated and sorted by score before being returned to the user. The END-TO-END-QA demo weaves these components together using the CFO framework (Chakravarti et al., 2019), which is a novel approach for orchestrating services.

5 Model Architecture

Our MRC QA model accepts a single query-document pair as its input and produces a span from the document along with a prediction score as its output. The underlying QA model is based on (Pan et al., 2019). The base layer of the QA system encodes the question and the candidate paragraph using the cross-lingual M-BERT (Devlin et al., 2019) and XLM-R (Conneau et al., 2019) representations. An output feed forward layer is added on top of the base layer to produce 3 sets of scores: scores at each token offset marking the likelihood of an answer chunk (1) starting at this offset, (2) ending at this offset, and (3) the entire sequence marking the likelihood of the question being answerable given the current context.

6 Experiments

We experiment with several multi-lingual models on the MLQA test set prior to integration in our system. We explore zero-shot learning as in prior work (Lewis et al., 2019) by training and fine-tuning on SQUAD 1.1 (Rajpurkar et al., 2016) for M-BERT and the XLM-R QA models. Refer to (Chakravarti et al., 2019; Pan et al., 2019) for additional details about model architecture and implementation. We train our models using the Huggingface code[8] with the default parameters except 3e-5 learning rate, 2 training epochs, 32 batch size and, 790 warmup steps.

We show results for the cross-lingual task (XLT), where the question and context are in the same language (e.g. question (q) and context (c) in Chinese) on the left side of Table 1. We find that our comparable re-implementations of models reported in prior work (Lewis et al., 2019) perform significantly better. We expect the improvement is due to using the Hugging Face implementation and hyper-parameter tuning values. Our best results using XLM-R large are consistently as strong as prior work in all languages. We also show results for the generalized cross-lingual task (G-XLT) where the question and context are in different languages in Table 1; XLM-R large achieves the best results in this experiment as well. We also compare the performance of the multilingual models with the performance of the English ROBERTA large model on the English MLQA dataset and find the results are similar.

We also provide additional analysis for the MLQA results by showing the difference per each question type in Table 2, for the XLT task. Having this information is useful for understanding which question types should be explored in more detail. We notice that the XLM-R$_L$ performance is more stable across all question types. All systems obtain the best performance for the "when" questions and the lowest for the "why" questions. We expect this is because "why" questions are more of an explanation making them more challenging while "when" questions tend to be easier because they are usually dates or numbers. We determine the question type by examining the English questions. Since MLQA has parallel examples, we used the question id to determine the question type when the question is in different languages.

Further, we show the value of having a multilingual model by also exploring QA for COVID-19 using the CORD-19 (Wang et al., 2020; Tang et al., 2020) dataset on English and translated data in Spanish and Chinese. The ability to answers questions in other languages is especially important in this use-case

---

[8] https://github.com/huggingface/transformers

F1	who	why	where	what	how	which	when	other	avg
M-BERT	64.6	44.2	54.9	61.9	62.4	62.6	**64.9**	61.0	61.8
XLM-R$_B$	68.4	56.9	60.7	63.3	67.4	64.1	**75.9**	65.5	65.1
XLM-R$_L$	76.5	66.7	68.9	70.9	74.4	71.9	**81.7**	71.9	72.7

Table 2: F1 score on the MLQA test set for the cross-lingual transfer task (XLT). Training data is SQUAD 1.1. B is the Base model and L is the Large model. The best performing question types are shown in **bold**. We also include the XLT averages from Table 1 for comparison.

Context	Question	# Examples	T_{GPU}	T_{CPU}
hi	ar	186	50	721
en	de	512	35	1525
zh	hi	189	61	628
en	ar	517	69	1215
zh	ar	188	57	615

Table 3: Dev Set Performance on MLQA benchmarked on the CPU and GPU. Times in seconds.

because the corpus is rapidly growing and some papers may only be available in a single language. The results are shown on the right side of Table 1. Although the overall performance is lower than MLQA, results are consistent across languages. XLM-R is still the best performing model. In contrast to passage level QA in MLQA and SQUAD, the CORD-19 dataset is document level. We expect this causes a large detriment to the performance.

Finally, while the best performing model is XLM-R large, there is merit to including the M-BERT model in the demo due to its reduced size which makes deployment more scalable. We use our M-BERT model for runtime experiments. A single x86-64 Intel® core is used as the CPU whereas one Nvidia® Tesla® V100 is used as the GPU. For brevity we show results for a random subset of five context question language pairs in Table 3. As expected running the model on GPU is faster than CPU: on average a given language pair is processed 19 times faster on GPU than CPU as shown in Table 3. The GPU also produces more consistent runtimes than CPU: standard deviation in CPU runtimes for each language pair is 32 times more than on GPU. We also find that not all languages decode equally quickly. Language pairs including English, particularly as the context, are the quickest to decode on GPU. Chinese and Hindi contexts take 2 to 3 times as long. The same trend holds on CPU, where the multiplier is approximately 1.5. Additionally, these differences are not fully explained by differing context sizes. On average Chinese and Hindi contexts are 1.4 and 0.9 times as long as their English counterparts respectively as seen in Table 4 of (Lewis et al., 2019). Question sizes are an order to two of magnitude shorter than contexts. This indicates that some languages decode faster than others even when accounting for context sizes.

7 Conclusion

In this paper we present our M-GAAMA demo, an interface for interacting with our multilingual QA MRC system. To the best of our knowledge we are the first to present a QA demo with multilingual capabilities in over 100 languages. We enable the user to be able to ask a question in one language, find the answer in another language, and with the use of machine translation the user can see the answer in the question language or another desired language. We also show how M-GAAMA can be used in a downstream task in our END-TO-END-QA demo. Finally, we show that our system achieves results that are consistently as strong as prior work on the MLQA dataset (Lewis et al., 2019) using XLM-R-Large on all seven languages. It can also be used to perform QA in current events via the CORD-19 COVID-19 (Wang et al., 2020; Tang et al., 2020) dataset. In the future we plan on experimenting with additional QA datsets such as Natural Questions (Kwiatkowski et al., 2019) and TyDiQA (Clark et al., 2020).

8   Acknowledgements

We would like to thank Andy Sakrajda for the help with IBM Watson Translation pipeline and Vittorio Castelli and Cezar Pendus with the help in building the multiligual search corpus. We would also like to thank the authors of the MLQA and XLM-R paper for helping us by sharing the hyper-parameters to repeat some of their experiments and help us while we debug the XLM-R models for Chinese.

References

Rishav Chakravarti, Cezar Pendus, Andrzej Sakrajda, Anthony Ferritto, Lin Pan, Michael Glass, Vittorio Castelli, J William Murdock, Radu Florian, Salim Roukos, and Avirup Sil. 2019. CFO: A framework for building production nlp systems. *EMNLP-IJCNLP, Demo Track*.

Jonathan H. Clark, Eunsol Choi, Michael Collins, Dan Garrette, Tom Kwiatkowski, Vitaly Nikolaev, and Jennimaria Palomaki. 2020. Tydi qa: A benchmark for information-seeking question answering in typologically diverse languages. *TACL*.

Alexis Conneau, Kartikay Khandelwal, Naman Goyal, Vishrav Chaudhary, Guillaume Wenzek, Francisco Guzmán, Edouard Grave, Myle Ott, Luke Zettlemoyer, and Veselin Stoyanov. 2019. Unsupervised cross-lingual representation learning at scale. *arXiv preprint arXiv:1911.02116*.

Jacob Devlin, Ming-Wei Chang, Kenton Lee, and Kristina Toutanova. 2019. BERT: Pre-training of deep bidirectional transformers for language understanding. In *NAACL-HLT*.

Tom Kwiatkowski, Jennimaria Palomaki, Olivia Redfield, Michael Collins, Ankur Parikh, Chris Alberti, Danielle Epstein, Illia Polosukhin, Matthew Kelcey, Jacob Devlin, Kenton Lee, Kristina N. Toutanova, Llion Jones, Ming-Wei Chang, Andrew Dai, Jakob Uszkoreit, Quoc Le, and Slav Petrov. 2019. Natural Questions: a benchmark for question answering research. *TACL*.

Guillaume Lample and Alexis Conneau. 2019. Cross-lingual language model pretraining. *Advances in Neural Information Processing Systems (NeurIPS)*.

Patrick Lewis, Barlas Ouz, Ruty Rinott, Sebastian Riedel, and Holger Schwenk. 2019. Mlqa: Evaluating cross-lingual extractive question answering.

Yinhan Liu, Myle Ott, Naman Goyal, Jingfei Du, Mandar Joshi, Danqi Chen, Omer Levy, Mike Lewis, Luke Zettlemoyer, and Veselin Stoyanov. 2019. RoBERTa: A robustly optimized BERT pretraining approach. *CoRR*.

Marco Lui and Timothy Baldwin. 2012. langid.py: An off-the-shelf language identification tool. In *Proceedings of the ACL 2012 System Demonstrations*, pages 25–30, Jeju Island, Korea, July. ACL.

Lin Pan, Rishav Chakravarti, Anthony Ferritto, Michael Glass, Alfio Gliozzo, Salim Roukos, Radu Florian, and Avirup Sil. 2019. Frustratingly easy natural question answering.

Pranav Rajpurkar, Jian Zhang, Konstantin Lopyrev, and Percy Liang. 2016. SQuAD: 100,000+ questions for machine comprehension of text. *EMNLP*.

Pranav Rajpurkar, Robin Jia, and Percy Liang. 2018. Know what you don't know: Unanswerable questions for SQuAD. *arXiv preprint arXiv:1806.03822*.

Varun Talvar. 2016. grpc design and implementation, 5. Talk by Varun Talwar, Product Manager at Google at Stanford, California [Accessed: 2019 06 20].

Raphael Tang, Rodrigo Nogueira, Edwin M. Zhang, Nikhil Gupta, Phng Ths. Bùi Cm, Kyunghyun Cho, and Jimmy Lin. 2020. Rapidly bootstrapping a question answering dataset for covid-19. *ArXiv*, abs/2004.11339.

Ashish Vaswani, Noam Shazeer, Niki Parmar, Jakob Uszkoreit, Llion Jones, Aidan N Gomez, Ł ukasz Kaiser, and Illia Polosukhin. 2017. Attention is all you need. In *NeurIPS*. Curran Associates, Inc.

Lucy Lu Wang, Kyle Lo, Yoganand Chandrasekhar, Russell Reas, Jiangjiang Yang, Darrin Eide, Kathryn Funk, Rodney Michael Kinney, Ziyang Liu, William. Merrill, Paul Mooney, Dewey A. Murdick, Devvret Rishi, Jerry Sheehan, Zhihong Shen, Brandon Stilson, Alex D. Wade, Kuansan Wang, Christopher Wilhelm, Boya Xie, Douglas M. Raymond, Daniel S. Weld, Oren Etzioni, and Sebastian Kohlmeier. 2020. Cord-19: The covid-19 open research dataset. *ArXiv*.

Peilin Yang, Hui Fang, and Jimmy Lin. 2017. Anserini: Enabling the use of lucene for information retrieval research. SIGIR. ACM.

Zhilin Yang, Peng Qi, Saizheng Zhang, Yoshua Bengio, William W Cohen, Ruslan Salakhutdinov, and Christopher D Manning. 2018. HotpotQA: A dataset for diverse, explainable multi-hop question answering. *arXiv preprint arXiv:1809.09600.*

Wei Yang, Yuqing Xie, Aileen Lin, Xingyu Li, Luchen Tan, Kun Xiong, Ming Li, and Jimmy Lin. 2019. End-to-end open-domain question answering with bertserini.

XplaiNLI: Explainable Natural Language Inference through Visual Analytics

Aikaterini-Lida Kalouli[1], **Rita Sevastjanova**[1], **Valeria de Paiva**[2],
Richard Crouch[3], and **Mennatallah El-Assady**[1]
[1] University of Konstanz, `firstname.lastname@uni.kn`
[2] Topos Institute, `valeria.depaiva@gmail.com`
[3] Chegg, `dick.crouch@gmail.com`

Abstract

Advances in Natural Language Inference (NLI) have helped us understand what state-of-the-art models really learn and what their generalization power is. Recent research has revealed some heuristics and biases of these models. However, to date, there is no systematic effort to capitalize on those insights through a system that uses these to *explain* the NLI decisions. To this end, we propose XplaiNLI, an eXplainable, interactive, visualization interface that computes NLI with different methods and provides explanations for the decisions made by the different approaches.

1 Introduction

We present XplaiNLI, an interactive visualization, web-based interface that computes Natural Language Inference (NLI) with three different approaches and provides sketches of explanations for the decision made by each approach.[1] An overview of XplaiNLI is found in Figure 1. The user on the frontend (right) inputs a premise (P) and a hypothesis (H). The pair is passed to the backend (left) where it goes through a symbolic and a deep learning (DL) component, which compute an inference label each. Each component also determines the rules and features that lead to the decision: for the symbolic one, we use Natural Logic (Valencia, 1991) inference rules to explain the inference label, while for the DL approach, we use insights gained from relevant work (Naik et al., 2018; Gururangan et al., 2018; Dasgupta et al., 2018; McCoy et al., 2019) to account for the decision. The complete output enters the hybrid component, which combines the strengths of the symbolic NLI engine and the DL model and determines which approach's label should be trusted based on semantic characteristics of the sentences. All output is forwarded to the frontend, where an intuitive visualization encodes the inference labels of the three approaches as well the corresponding explanations. The user can interact further with the interface by adding her own heuristics and by providing feedback on the inference label, which is used for improving the separate components.

2 Related Work

Work on interpretability for NLI is still at an early stage. One strand of research explains the models by "stress-testing" them and revealing the phenomena that the models cannot handle or by detecting bias in the training data (Gururangan et al., 2018; Dasgupta et al., 2018; McCoy et al., 2019, inter alia). Another strand of research has approached the task by directly learning natural language explanations along with the inference decision (Camburu et al., 2018) or creating distributional representations of syntactic and semantic inference rules (Zanzotto and Ferrone, 2017) and training machine-learning models on them. Although all these approaches shed light on the processes behind the reasoning task, the insights gained have not yet been used in their full potential; XplaiNLI seeks to fill this gap.

3 XplaiNLI Backend Model

The backend outputs the inference relation for a given pair, as well as the features that lead to that decision, based on each of the following three approaches. The exact backend implementation and the performance

[1] Video: `dropbox.com/s/mbgn3u6ilngohe1/XplaiNLI.mp4?dl=0` Demo: `bit.ly/XplaiNLI` Code: `https://github.com/kkalouli/XplaiNLI`

Proceedings of the 27th International Conference on Computational Linguistics, pages 48–52
Barcelona, Spain (Online), December 12, 2020.

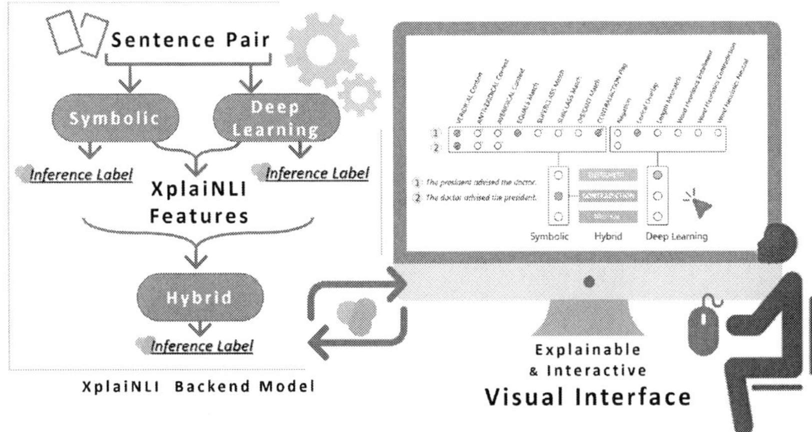

Figure 1: The high-level architecture of XplaiNLI: on the left, the three NLI approaches providing an inference label and explainable features, and on the right, the interactive, explainable, visual frontend.

of each of the approaches is detailed in Kalouli et al. (2020); this paper focuses on explainability.

3.1 The Deep Learning Component

For the DL component we use BERT-base (Devlin et al., 2018), one of the state-of-the-art models for NLI, which we fine-tune for our task. For fine-tuning, we use the SemEval 2014 version of SICK (Marelli et al., 2014). We utilize a corrected version of the corpus (Kalouli et al., 2018)[2] to mitigate some of the shortcomings of the original corpus, e.g., event and entity coreference issues. We do not fine-tune on other commonly-used benchmarks, such as MNLI (Williams et al., 2017), as these corpora suffer from similar problems. For fine-tuning, we use the HuggingFace implementation[3] and we fine-tune the parameters suggested by the authors: batch size, learning rate and number of epochs. Our best performing model uses a batch size of 32, learning rate of 2e-5 and 3 epochs. The trained model classifies an input pair into E(ntailment), C(ontradiction) or N(eutral).

To provide *potential* explanations for the model's decision, we implement the findings of Naik et al. (2018), Gururangan et al. (2018), Dasgupta et al. (2018) and McCoy et al. (2019). Their work has revealed specific heuristics and artifacts that arguably appear in the training sets of these models and can thus explain to some extent the way the models label a pair. Particularly, we implement four kinds of heuristics/explanations. First, the presence of negation. As observed by Naik et al. (2018), Dasgupta et al. (2018) and McCoy et al. (2019), negation words such as *no, not, don't, nobody*, etc. make the model predict C, consistent with the heuristic found in the SNLI training set. Second, we follow Dasgupta et al. (2018), Naik et al. (2018) and McCoy et al. (2019) and compute the lexical overlap of the two sentences. It is argued that whenever H is completely contained in P, the models tend to predict E, no matter the word order or other constraints. The third heuristic of sentence length is similar (Naik et al., 2018; Gururangan et al., 2018): Hs that are much longer than their Ps tend to be neutral, while Hs that are shorter than their Ps tend to be entailed. Last, we add relation-specific word heuristics. According to the findings of Gururangan et al. (2018), specific words being present in H or/and P are characteristic for a specific inference relation. So, generic words like *animal, instrument, outdoors* are mostly found in the Hs of entailments, while modifiers and superlatives like *sad, tall, best, first* are mostly found in neutral pairs.

3.2 The Symbolic Component

The symbolic component implements a version of *Natural Logic* (NL) (Valencia, 1991). NL attempts to explain inferences through monotonicity, i.e., by whether the concepts expressed in a sentence can become "more general" or "more specific" salva veritate. For example, in the sentence *a woman is walking, woman*

---

[2]Available under `github.com/kkalouli/SICK-processing`
[3]Available under `github.com/huggingface/transformers`

can be replaced by the more general *person* while preserving truth. The symbolic component is based on an improved version of the Graphical Knowledge Representation (GKR) by Kalouli and Crouch (2018) – GKR allows for the kind of inference mechanism we require. In the first stage of the process, P and H are parsed to their GKR representations, each producing six default GKR graphs: a dependency graph, a conceptual graph, a contextual graph, a lexical graph, a properties graph and a coreference graph. In the next stage, the lexical graphs, which contain, for each content word, the WordNet (Fellbaum, 1998) senses, synonyms, antonyms, hypernyms, hyponyms and the SUMO (Niles and Pease, 2001) concepts, superconcepts and subconcepts are used to determine matches between H and P and their specificity. For example, *person* in H can be matched to *woman* in P and be assigned the specificity *superclass*: *person* is a hypernym of *woman*. One of the four specificity markers (*equal, subclass, superclass, disjoint*) can be assigned. In the next stage, the determined specificities are updated based on the predicate-argument structure of each sentence, captured in the concept graph. For instance, *woman* is a subclass of *person* but it is not a subclass of *tall person* (not all women are tall). For the two terms of a match, the system considers if both, none or only one of them have dependents (modifiers/arguments) in their respective concept graph. Based on that, different update rules apply. For example, if *person* in H has additional dependents such as *tall* but *woman* in P does not, then the match becomes more specific: since H (*person*) was already more general than P (*woman*) (specificity superclass), then making this match more specific leads to the specificity becoming undetermined (none). After updating all H-P matches, the exact inference relation is determined based on the GKR context graphs, the instantiabilities they contain and the specificities of the matches. For example, if the H-term is instantiated and more or equally specific than the uninstantiated P-term (*a woman – no woman*), there is a contradiction. If the H-term is instantiated and more general (*a person – no woman*) than the P-term, we cannot determine the relation. Similarly for entailments: if the match is equally or more specific and both terms are instantiated, there is an entailment (*a woman - a woman*. See Kalouli et al. (2020) for more details on the symbolic engine.

These rules, i.e. the exact combinations of specificity relations and contexts, can be used straight-forwardly to explain the decision made by the symbolic component.

3.3 The Hybrid Component

The hybrid approach is based on the fact that distributional features are suitable for dealing with conceptual aspects of the meanings of words, phrases, and sentences, but struggle with Boolean and contextual phenomena like modals, quantifiers, negation, implicatives, propositional attitudes, conditionals, etc. (Dasgupta et al., 2018; Naik et al., 2018; McCoy et al., 2019, to name only a few). These are phenomena to which more symbolic/structural approaches are well suited. Thus, we expect that "easy" cases which do not involve such phenomena will be best handled by the DL approach, while hard linguistic phenomena like the ones mentioned will be best handled by the symbolic approach. Thus, the hybrid component determines whether to use the symbolic or the DL label as its own inference label, based on specific semantic characteristics of the pair.

During training, the hybrid classifier learns for each pair which of the components delivers the right label (again based on the SICK-train corpus): the symbolic one (S), the DL one (DL) or both of them (B).[4] With this, the classifier indirectly learns whether the pair is "easy" or hard: if S is right, the pair is probably hard; if DL is right, the pair is probably easier; if both are right, we cannot make any claims about the nature of the pair. The learning is based on the implemented rules of the symbolic component (cf. Section 3.2), which are converted to features, e.g., the pair *P: The woman is walking. H: The person is not walking* would be assigned the features *veridical, antiveridical, superclass* because the match *person-woman* has the superclass specificity and the highest match *walk-walk* is instantiated in P and uninstantiated in H. These features (rules) capture the effects of hard linguistic phenomena like modals, negation, quantifiers, implicatives, factives, etc. To target explainability and as decision trees have been shown to be one of the most interpretable models (Guidotti et al., 2018), we train a Random Forest classifier (Gini impurity) with 30 estimators:[5] each pair is classified as one of S, DL or B, and then mapped to the respective label: if

---

[4] If none of them delivers the right label, then we cannot make any claims about the nature of the pair.

[5] This classifier is different from the one in Kalouli et al. (2020), where the focus is on performance rather than explainability.

classified as S or DL, the symbolic or the DL inference label are used, respectively; if classified as B, then either one of S or DL can be chosen but we use the DL label for higher robustness.

The features used for prediction are also used for explainability purposes.

4 Explainable Visual Interface

The user interface (Figure 1, right) features three main components, all emphasizing the role of the human-in-the-loop. Two text fields (for P and H) allow users to insert the inference pair to be computed.

Visualizing Explanations With the submission of the input pair, the system on the backend computes one inference label for each approach as well as explanations for each label. The results are visualized with an intuitive visualization schema (Figure 1, right): each sentence of the pair is presented along with all features that could lead to a certain inference label. On the left side, the user can find the features (rules) of the symbolic approach and on the right, the features of the DL model. The features that are relevant for this pair are colored and contain ✓, if the feature's value is true, or no ✓, if the value is false. The color of the features encodes the inference relation that each approach predicted: green is for E, red for C and grey for N. Some DL features might have lower opacity: this means that they should – according to the literature – lead to a different label than the one actually predicted by the model. In this way, the user can verify previous literature findings or discover new patterns. The colored features are then linked with the predicted inference label, also encoded by color. No link between the DL features and the label means that the prediction is not based on any of these features. In the middle of the visualization, the user can find the label of the hybrid approach, marked with bold text. Again, links visualize the behavior of the approach: if there is a link between the symbolic decision and the hybrid one, the hybrid approach chose the symbolic label; if the link is between the DL label and the hybrid one, the hybrid approach chose the DL label. If both links exist, then the labels of symbolic and DL were the same and so the hybrid approach just chose one of them. In terms of visualization, all features used for the hybrid decision are marked with a grey H in increasing opacity: the darker the color, the more weight this feature had for the decision.

User-defined Heuristics Along with the input pair, users can also input words – also words not found in P or H – that are expected to act as heuristics for a certain inference relation. The option of input words is available for both P and H and for all three inference relations. For instance, the user can insert the word *asleep* in the `Contradiction` field of H to check the artifact that hypotheses containing the word *asleep* are bound to be labeled as C by a DL model. Due to the system's architecture (see Section 3), only the DL model might get explained by additional heuristics; the symbolic approach is based on predefined inference rules and the hybrid approach uses semantic features to make its decision, independently from surface heuristics. The current version of the system only supports the search for specific words as heuristics; future versions will extend to further user-defined heuristics, e.g. Part-Of-Speech tags.

Learning from User Feedback The labels of the hybrid decision are at the same time clickable buttons for users to provide their annotation of the pair. With this annotation, an (offline) learning process is initiated: the pair and the user's annotation are added to the training pool of the DL model so that the model can be re-trained on increasingly large data. Whenever enough data has been collected, the model is re-trained; this re-training also triggers the re-training of the hybrid model, leading to improved results.

5 Conclusion

This paper presented an interactive visualization interface for explainable NLI. The interface uses three different approaches to compute inference and visualizes the features that lead to each decision. In contrast to black-box machine-learning models, this approach enables users to get intuitions of the decision-making process (Spinner et al., 2020), as well as to distill linguistic knowledge about the analyzed phenomena. The options for user-defined heuristics and user-driven learning can help refine the used models and components and optimize them to the users' intuition and domain understanding. To increase explainability and comparability, future work will allow the user to a) choose between different DL models for training, b) choose between hybrid models trained on different datasets, c) define their own rules for the hybrid classifier, and d) display the decision tree of the hybrid classifier for better exploration.

References

Oana-Maria Camburu, Tim Rocktäschel, Thomas Lukasiewicz, and Phil Blunsom. 2018. e-snli: Natural language inference with natural language explanations. In *Advances in Neural Information Processing Systems*, pages 9539–9549.

Ishita Dasgupta, Demi Guo, Andreas Stuhlmüller, Samuel J. Gershman, and Noah D. Goodman. 2018. Evaluating Compositionality in Sentence Embeddings. *CoRR*, abs/1802.04302.

Jacob Devlin, Ming-Wei Chang, Kenton Lee, and Kristina Toutanova. 2018. BERT: Pre-training of Deep Bidirectional Transformers for Language understanding. *CoRR*, abs/1810.04805.

Christiane Fellbaum. 1998. *WordNet: An Electronic Lexical Database (Language, Speech, and Communication)*. The MIT Press.

Riccardo Guidotti, Anna Monreale, Salvatore Ruggieri, Franco Turini, Fosca Giannotti, and Dino Pedreschi. 2018. A Survey of Methods for Explaining Black Box Models. *ACM Comput. Surv.*, 51(5), August.

Suchin Gururangan, Swabha Swayamdipta, Omer Levy, Roy Schwartz, Samuel Bowman, and Noah A. Smith. 2018. Annotation Artifacts in Natural Language Inference Data. In *Proceedings of the 2018 Conference of the North American Chapter of the Association for Computational Linguistics: Human Language Technologies, Volume 2 (Short Papers)*, pages 107–112. Association for Computational Linguistics.

Aikaterini-Lida Kalouli and Richard Crouch. 2018. GKR: the Graphical Knowledge Representation for semantic parsing. In *Proceedings of the Workshop on Computational Semantics beyond Events and Roles*, pages 27–37, New Orleans, Louisiana. Association for Computational Linguistics.

Aikaterini-Lida Kalouli, Livy Real, and Valeria de Paiva. 2018. WordNet for "Easy" Textual Inferences. In *Proceedings of the Eleventh International Conference on Language Resources and Evaluation (LREC 2018)*, Paris, France, may. European Language Resources Association (ELRA).

Aikaterini-Lida Kalouli, Richard Crouch, and Valeria de Paiva. 2020. Hy-NLI: a Hybrid system for Natural Language Inference. In *Proceedings of the 28th International Conference on Computational Linguistics*, COLING '20. Association for Computational Linguistics.

Marco Marelli, Luisa Bentivogli, Marco Baroni, Raffaella Bernardi, Stefano Menini, and Roberto Zamparelli. 2014. SemEval-2014 Task 1: Evaluation of Compositional Distributional Semantic Models on Full Sentences through Semantic Relatedness and Textual Entailment. In *Proceedings of the 8th International Workshop on Semantic Evaluation (SemEval 2014)*, pages 1–8, Dublin, Ireland, August. Association for Computational Linguistics.

Tom McCoy, Ellie Pavlick, and Tal Linzen. 2019. Right for the wrong reasons: Diagnosing syntactic heuristics in natural language inference. In *Proceedings of the 57th Annual Meeting of the Association for Computational Linguistics*, pages 3428–3448, Florence, Italy, July. Association for Computational Linguistics.

Aakanksha Naik, Abhilasha Ravichander, Norman Sadeh, Carolyn Rose, and Graham Neubig. 2018. Stress Test Evaluation for Natural Language Inference. In *Proceedings of the 27th International Conference on Computational Linguistics*, pages 2340–2353, Santa Fe, New Mexico, USA, August. Association for Computational Linguistics.

Ian Niles and Adam Pease. 2001. Toward a Standard Upper Ontology. In Chris Welty and Barry Smith, editors, *Proceedings of the 2nd International Conference on Formal Ontology in Information Systems (FOIS-2001)*, pages 2–9.

Thilo Spinner, Udo Schlegel, Hannah Schäfer, and Menna El-Assady. 2020. explAIner: A Visual Analytics Framework for Interactive and Explainable Machine Learning. *IEEE Transactions on Visualization and Computer Graphics*, 26(1):1064–1074, Jan.

Victor Sánchez Valencia. 1991. *Studies on Natural Logic and Categorial Grammar*. Ph.D. thesis, University of Amsterdam.

Adina Williams, Nikita Nangia, and Samuel R. Bowman. 2017. A Broad-Coverage Challenge Corpus for Sentence Understanding through Inference. *CoRR*, abs/1704.05426.

F. M. Zanzotto and L. Ferrone. 2017. Can we explain natural language inference decisions taken with neural networks? Inference rules in distributed representations. In *2017 International Joint Conference on Neural Networks (IJCNN)*, pages 3680–3687, May.

Discussion Tracker: Supporting Teacher Learning about Students' Collaborative Argumentation in High School Classrooms

Luca Lugini and **Christopher Olshefski** and **Ravneet Singh** and
Diane Litman and **Amanda Godley**

University of Pittsburgh
Pittsburgh, PA, USA

Abstract

Teaching collaborative argumentation is an advanced skill that many K-12 teachers struggle to develop. To address this, we have developed Discussion Tracker, a classroom discussion analytics system based on novel algorithms for classifying argument moves, specificity, and collaboration. Results from a classroom deployment indicate that teachers found the analytics useful, and that the underlying classifiers perform with moderate to substantial agreement with humans.

1 Introduction

Collaborative argumentation in student dialogue is essential to individual learning as well as group problem-solving (Reznitskaya and Gregory, 2013). Strong collaborative argumentation is characterized by specific claims, supporting evidence, and reasoning about that evidence as well as by building upon, questioning, and debating ideas posed by others. However, teaching collaborative argumentation is an advanced skill that many high school teachers struggle to develop (Lampert et al., 2010), partially due to the practical challenge of keeping track of important features of students' talk while managing class and reflecting on students' talk when no record of it exists.

To address this challenge, we have developed Discussion Tracker (DT), a system that leverages natural language processing (NLP) to provide teachers with automatically generated data about three important dimensions of students' collaborative argumentation: argument moves, specificity and collaboration. Discussion Tracker includes visualizations, interactive coded transcripts, collaboration maps, analytics across discussions, and instructional planning. In contrast to teacher dashboards which largely focus on discussion analytics such as amount of student/teacher talk, teacher wait time, and teacher question type (Chen et al., 2014; Gerritsen et al., 2018; Pehmer et al., 2015; Blanchard et al., 2016), DT focuses on students' collaborative argumentation. In contrast to related NLP algorithms which largely focus on coding student essays (Ghosh et al., 2016; Klebanov et al., 2016; Nguyen and Litman, 2016), asynchronous online discussions (Swanson et al., 2015), and news articles (Li and Nenkova, 2015), DT's NLP algorithms address the challenges of coding transcripts of synchronous, face-to-face classroom discussions.

2 Description of Discussion Tracker (DT)

To use DT, a teacher first uploads a classroom discussion transcript. Next, NLP classifiers code the transcript using a previously developed scheme for representing three important dimensions of collaborative argumentation (Lugini et al., 2018; Olshefski et al., 2020): argument moves (claim, evidence, explanation), specificity (low, medium, high), and collaboration (new, agree, extension, challenge/probe). Student turns are the unit of analysis for collaboration. Argumentative Discourse Units (ADUs) — either entire turns, or segments within turns — are the argumentation and specificity units of analysis.

Each NLP classifier in DT was developed by training on a previously collected and freely available corpus[1] of collaborative argumentation (Olshefski et al., 2020) using transformer-based neural networks.

---

[1]`http://discussiontracker.cs.pitt.edu/` - we refer to this as corpus C1.

Proceedings of the 27th International Conference on Computational Linguistics, pages 53–58
Barcelona, Spain (Online), December 12, 2020.

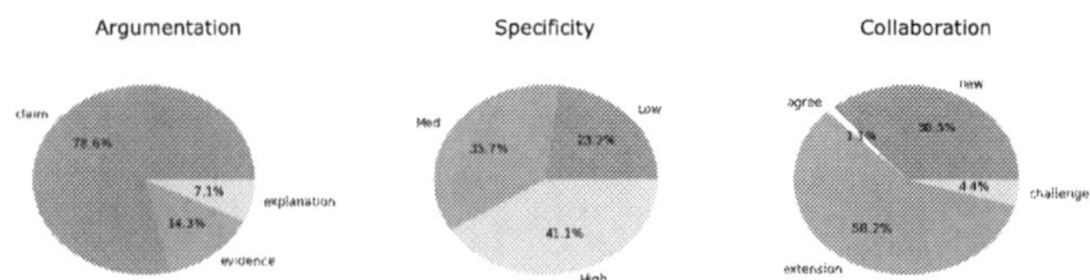

Figure 1: Partial screenshot of "Overview" page in Discussion Tracker.

Discussion Tracker

Current Discussion	Discussion History	Plan Next Discussion
Overview	Annotated Transcript · Collaboration Map	Help

Turn	Student	Talk	ArgMove	Specificity	Collaboration
1	teacher	alright so for the purpose of refresher give us a quick summary about this story. don't be shy.			
2	7	there was a grandfather who was a wwii survivor and he wanted his granddaughter to name, the child, her child after his grandson, but then she didn't and that kind of fractured the relationship.	claim	med	new
3	8	so like a lot of the middle of the story is about why he wants her to name the child after mandel and how the mother kind of gets to choose her opinion in this situation.	claim	med	extension
4	16	i also feel like this story talks a lot about the generational gap [inaudible 00:00:58].	claim	low	new
5	teacher	make sure you guys talk nice and loud today. alright someone give us a question that you have and if you could try to keep it chronological, as much as possible. try to do it quickly so that we can get a lot in today.			
6	1	all right i'll start off. um i think we should look into the character of the grandfather a bit. like how he has memory loss and he seems to cause he brings out these papers each time. um. i think we could summarize the character of what he's like.			non
7	5	so uh i think a big part of the grandfather's character is his pride. he's very proud of where he comes from and of his family and everything that they've done to, in their history.	claim	med	new
8	8	agreed, i feel the author also likes to stress the physical characteristic of the grandfather	claim	med	extension
		because often when he comes in he immediately describes his eyes and his face and his eyes are um shining sometimes and other times they've lost the shine	evidence	med	
		and i feel like the author indirectly wants you to know how the grandfather feels as soon as he enters the scene. and i think uh this importance, uh especially with, that you immediately know how he feels and it feels on and off sometimes where sometimes he has the shine in his eyes, sometimes he doesn't uh is very inconsistent about him and i think this plays into like the entire theme of the story in itself which was remembering past generations um. the fact that the grandfather cannot, maybe his motivation for wanting the, is it his grandson or great-great grandson uh to have the name to remember them by.	explanation	high	

Figure 2: Screenshot of "Annotated Transcript" page in Discussion Tracker.

A pretrained BERT model (Devlin et al., 2019; Wolf et al., 2019) is used to generate word embeddings for each word in an ADU (or turn, for collaboration). An average pooling layer is then used to compute the final embedding for the target ADU. For predicting specificity, a softmax classifier is applied to the target ADU embedding. For predicting argument moves, the target ADU as well as a window of surrounding ADUs are embedded, then concatenated to form the final feature vector. A softmax layer is applied on top of the feature vector to complete the argument move classifier. This improves our prior argumentation models (Lugini and Litman, 2018) by using a pre-trained neural network and adding context information (Lugini and Litman, 2020). The collaboration classifier is slightly more complex since collaboration labels depend on the relationship between a target turn and a particular reference turn. For the purpose of this work we assume that the target turn is already provided in the input transcript. A pretrained BERT model and average pooling layer are used to generate embeddings for the target and reference turns. An element-wise multiplication between the two embeddings is performed, yielding the feature vector used by a softmax classifier.

All models use the *bert-base-uncased* BERT variant from the HuggingFace (Wolf et al., 2019) library, which results in the smallest available dimensionality to keep computational complexity to a minimum. The three models were built using the Keras library (Chollet and others, 2015). The *Adam* optimizer was used, as well as early stopping to automatically determine the number of epochs for training by monitoring validation loss (the validation set was chosen randomly and consisted of 10% of the initial training set for each fold).

After classification, all discussion analytics are automatically generated from the NLP codes. The DT overview screen (Figure 1) includes pie charts indicating the distribution of the codes for students' argument moves, specificity, and collaboration. Other screens include interactive coded transcripts (Figure 2), collaboration maps (Figure 3), identification of strengths and weaknesses to support teacher goal-setting (Figure 4), and a history page (not shown) that compares the code distributions across discussions.

We initially implemented a desktop version of DT using Python and Tkinter. The screenshots in the figures and the usability evaluation below are based on this version. To make DT more portable across hardware and to allow teachers to easily use DT on multiple machines (e.g., school, home), we now have

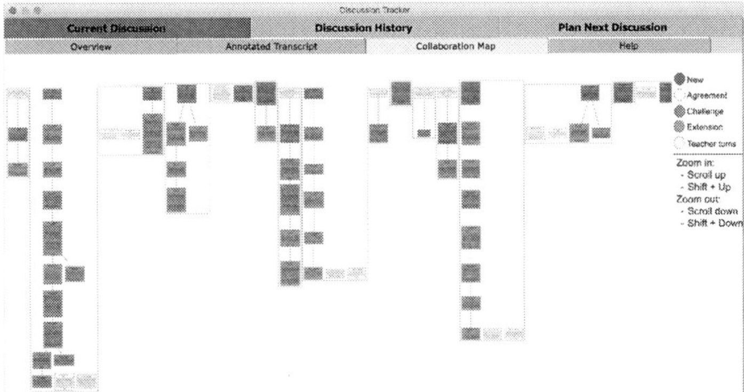

Figure 3: Screenshot of "Collaboration Map" page in Discussion Tracker.

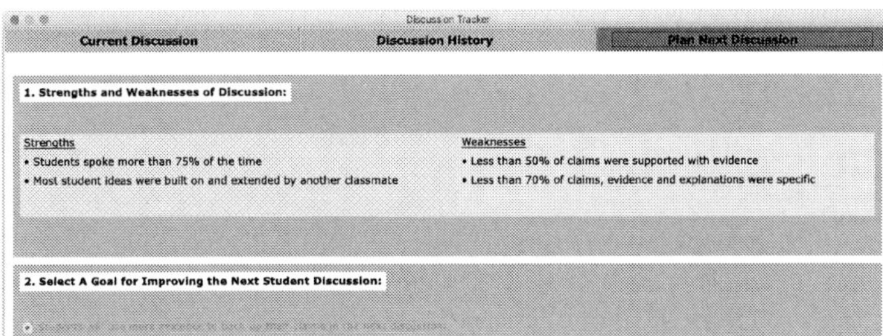

Figure 4: Partial screenshot of "Plan Next Discussion" page in Discussion Tracker.

a web version of DT[2]. This version is implemented in Python and uses the REMI package[3] to convert Python into HTML and launch a webserver to accept requests for the site and handle user input. With this setup it is easy to integrate the classifiers, implemented as a REST API on the same server hosting .

3   Evaluation

From January to March 2020, we collected data (corpus C2) to evaluate both teacher perceptions of DT as well as NLP classifier performance. In particular, the desktop version of DT was used by 18 high school English Language Arts teachers from 4 schools, where: 1) each teacher led a discussion about a literary text that was audio-recorded and observed by a researcher, 2) each teacher completed an online survey within a day, 3) experienced annotators[4] hand-coded transcripts of the discussion for the three dimensions of collaborative argumentation discussed above and uploaded them into the DT system, 4) within two weeks, researchers conducted a 45-minute cognitive interview (Voet and Wever, 2017) with each teacher while they were using DT to look at their students' discussion[5], and 5) the same day, teachers completed a second survey that mirrored the first with additional items for ratings of DT.

DT Usability. We measured teachers' perceptions of the overall usefulness of DT and of specific features/visualizations through Likert-scale items on the survey from step 5 above. Survey items were based on Holden and Rada's (2011) teacher survey of perceived usability of technology. To remove noise that might distract from this usability evaluation, we evaluated DT under the best possible NLP conditions by using the manual codings of collaborative argumentation from step 3 above to generate all analytics. The NLP codings are separately evaluated in the classifier discussion below. Table 1 indicates that teachers perceived DT to be very helpful for their learning about facilitating collaborative argumentation. For nine of the 13 items, all teachers selected either "Agree" or "Strongly agree" (a mean score of 4.5), and no item received a "Strongly disagree." Although the item "I find the system easy to

---

[2]Web app demo link and details and source at `discussiontracker.cs.pitt.edu`
[3]`https://github.com/dddomodossola/remi`
[4]Kappa for argumentation (0.971) and collaboration (0.578) and Quadratic Weighted Kappa for specificity (0.813).
[5]Teachers navigated DT with minimal training (a 15-minute, face-to-face demo).

Question	Mean	Question	Mean
The overview of the discussion is helpful.	4.67	I find the system easy to use.	4.11
The pie charts of different features of the student discussion are helpful.	4.78	The system helps me to recognize my students' strengths during discussion.	4.72
The annotated transcript of student discussion is helpful.	4.89	The system helps me to recognize my students' weakness during discussion.	4.72
The collaboration diagram is helpful.	4.22	The system gives me more insight into student learning than I usually get from thinking about the discussion.	4.67
The system-generated strengths and weaknesses are helpful.	4.44	The system encourages me to make more changes to my facilitation of discussion than I usually do.	4.28
The goal-setting is helpful.	4.56	Overall, Discussion Tracker is helpful for my teaching of literature discussions.	4.72
The instructional resources are helpful.	4.17		

Table 1: Teacher survey items and Likert score means.

Annotation	Distribution
Argumentation	claim (72%), evidence (18%), explanation (10%)
Specificity	low (29%), medium (36%), high (36%)
Collaboration	new (22%), agree (3%), extensions (54%), challenge/probe (21%)

Table 2: Descriptive statistics of gold-standard annotations in test corpus.

Code	N	Kappa	Macro F	Micro F
Argument Move	1942 ADUs	0.574	0.730	0.789
Specificity	1942 ADUs	0.727	0.688	0.679
Collaboration	1467 Turns	0.566	0.439	0.775

Table 3: Transfomer-based neural classification results.

use" received the lowest score (4.11), all teachers either agreed or agreed strongly with the item. Other items that scored higher, however, varied more in responses. For example, although the majority of teachers agreed with "The collaboration diagram is helpful," three neither agreed nor disagreed.

NLP Classifier Performance. As the gold standard for evaluating DT classifier performance, we used the manual annotations from step 3 of the data collection discussed above. Table 2 shows the distribution of the gold-standard codes, while Table 3 shows classifier performance when compared to these gold-standards.[6] The results in Table 3 were obtained by training each classifier separately on corpus C1 (footnote 1) and testing on corpus C2 (the 18 discussions collected in this study). Hyperparameter optimization was performed using cross-validation on C1 in order to find out how much contextual information before/after the target ADU to consider (i.e. context window size). This yielded an argument classifier that added a window of 2 ADUs preceding and 2 ADUs following the target ADU for embedding. Though all classifiers show respectable results, predictions for argument move and specificity are more consistent for individual class labels, as evidenced by the small difference between macro and micro F-score. The lower macro F-score for collaboration is due to poor prediction performance for the agree and challenge/probe codes.

---

[6]The input for the gold-standard and automated coding was identical (loosely, a spreadsheet version of the first three columns in Figure 2). A professional service (rather than ASR) performed the audio transcription and segmentation into turns (for collaboration coding). A researcher further segmented student turns into ADUs (for argumentation and specificity coding).

4   Summary and Future Directions

In this work we described the development of a classroom analytics system and reported usability results from real world classroom deployment. We conducted a survey that showed teachers found the system easy to use and the analytics (based on human-annotated labels) helpful in analyzing collaborative argumentation. Evaluation of the automated NLP classifiers showed that they are in moderate to substantial agreement with the labels provided by human annotators. The main goal of future work is to continue to enhance our neural classification methods, and to develop an end-to-end, completely automated system. To this end, we will consider several aspects: perform new data collections and improve classifier performance; incorporate Automatic Speech Recognition to perform automated transcription; develop algorithms to automatically segment turns into ADUs. In addition, we will further develop the interface by addressing teacher feedback and improving the system's ease of use. Finally, teachers will evaluate our newer versions of DT, including versions where the analytics are based on classifier outputs rather than human-annotated labels.

Acknowledgements

This work was supported by the National Science Foundation (1842334 and 1917673) and by the University of Pittsburgh's Learning Research and Development Center as well as Center for Research Computing through the resources provided. We would like to thank the teachers who participated in this study.

References

Nathaniel Blanchard, Patrick J Donnelly, Andrew M Olney, Borhan Samei, Brooke Ward, Xiaoyi Sun, Sean Kelly, Martin Nystrand, and Sidney K. D'Mello. 2016. Identifying teacher questions using automatic speech recognition in classrooms. In *17th Annual Meeting of the Special Interest Group on Discourse and Dialogue*, page 191.

G Chen, SN Clarke, and LB Resnick. 2014. An analytic tool for supporting teachers' reflection on classroom talk. In *Learning and becoming in practice: The International Conference of the Learning Sciences (ICLS) 2014*. International Society of the Learning Sciences.

François Chollet et al. 2015. Keras. `https://keras.io`.

Jacob Devlin, Ming-Wei Chang, Kenton Lee, and Kristina Toutanova. 2019. BERT: Pre-training of deep bidirectional transformers for language understanding. In *Proceedings of the 2019 Conference of the North American Chapter of the Association for Computational Linguistics: Human Language Technologies*, pages 4171–4186, Minneapolis, Minnesota, June.

David Gerritsen, John Zimmerman, and Amy Ogan. 2018. Towards a framework for smart classrooms that teach instructors to teach. In *International Conference of the Learning Sciences*, volume 3.

Debanjan Ghosh, Aquila Khanam, Yubo Han, and Smaranda Muresan. 2016. Coarse-grained Argumentation Features for Scoring Persuasive Essays. In *Proceedings of the 54th Annual Meeting of the Association for Computational Linguistics (Volume 2: Short Papers)*, pages 549–554.

Heather Holden and Roy Rada. 2011. Understanding the influence of perceived usability and technology self-efficacy on teachers' technology acceptance. *Journal of Research on Technology in Education*, 43(4):343–367.

Beata Beigman Klebanov, Christian Stab, Jill Burstein, Yi Song, Binod Gyawali, and Iryna Gurevych. 2016. Argumentation: Content, Structure, and Relationship with Essay Quality. In *Proceedings of the Third Workshop on Argument Mining (ArgMining2016)*, pages 70–75, Berlin, Germany.

Magdalene Lampert, Heather Beasley, Hala Ghousseini, Elham Kazemi, and Megan Franke. 2010. Using designed instructional activities to enable novices to manage ambitious mathematics teaching. In *Instructional explanations in the disciplines*, pages 129–141. Springer.

Junyi Jessy Li and Ani Nenkova. 2015. Fast and accurate prediction of sentence specificity. In *Proceedings of the Twenty-Ninth Conference on Artificial Intelligence (AAAI)*, pages 2281–2287, January.

Luca Lugini and Diane Litman. 2018. Argument component classification for classroom discussions. In *Proceedings of the 5th Workshop on Argument Mining*, pages 57–67.

Luca Lugini and Diane Litman. 2020. Contextual argument component classification for class discussions. In *Proceedings s of the 28th International Conference on Computational Linguistics*, Online, December.

Luca Lugini, Diane Litman, Amanda Godley, and Christopher Olshefski. 2018. Annotating student talk in text-based classroom discussions. In *Proceedings of the Thirteenth Workshop on Innovative Use of NLP for Building Educational Applications*, pages 110–116.

Huy Nguyen and Diane Litman. 2016. Context-aware Argumentative Relation Mining. In *Proceedings of the 54th Annual Meeting of the Association for Computational Linguistics (Volume 1: Long Papers)*, pages 1127–1137, Berlin, Germany.

Christopher Olshefski, Luca Lugini, Ravneet Singh, Diane Litman, and Amanda Godley. 2020. The Discussion Tracker corpus of collaborative argumentation. In *Proceedings of the 12th International Conference on Language Resources and Evaluation*, pages 1033–1043, Marseille, France, May.

Ann-Kathrin Pehmer, Alexander Gröschner, and Tina Seidel. 2015. How teacher professional development regarding classroom dialogue affects students' higher-order learning. *Teaching and Teacher Education*, 47:108–119.

Alina Reznitskaya and Maughn Gregory. 2013. Student thought and classroom language: Examining the mechanisms of change in dialogic teaching. *Educational Psychologist*, 48(2):114–133.

Reid Swanson, Brian Ecker, and Marilyn Walker. 2015. Argument mining: Extracting arguments from online dialogue. In *Proceedings of the 16th Annual Meeting of the Special Interest Group on Discourse and Dialogue*, pages 217–226.

Michiel Voet and Bram De Wever. 2017. History teachers' knowledge of inquiry methods: An analysis of cognitive processes used during a historical inquiry. *Journal of Teacher Education*, 68(3):312–329.

Thomas Wolf, Lysandre Debut, Victor Sanh, Julien Chaumond, Clement Delangue, Anthony Moi, Pierric Cistac, Tim Rault, R'emi Louf, Morgan Funtowicz, and Jamie Brew. 2019. Huggingface's transformers: State-of-the-art natural language processing. *ArXiv*, abs/1910.03771.

An Online Readability Leveled Arabic Thesaurus

Zhengyang Jiang, Nizar Habash, Muhamed Al Khalil
Computational Approaches to Modeling Language (CAMeL) Lab
New York University Abu Dhabi
{zj522,nizar.habash,muhamed.alkhalil}@nyu.edu

Abstract

This demo paper introduces the online Readability Leveled Arabic Thesaurus interface. For a given user input word, this interface provides the word's possible lemmas, roots, English glosses, related Arabic words and phrases, and readability on a five-level readability scale. This interface builds on and connects multiple existing Arabic resources and processing tools. This one-of-a-kind system enables Arabic speakers and learners to benefit from advances in Arabic computational linguistics technologies. Feedback from users of the system will help the developers to identify lexical coverage gaps and errors.

1 Introduction

Arabic is one of the six UN official languages, the language of millions of people in the Arab world, as well as the liturgy language of Muslims. It is also a language known for its difficulty for new learners; and its Modern Standard Arabic (MSA) form used in education and the media is technically not the native form spoken by modern-day Arabs, who speak a variety of its dialects. As such, there is a great need to have user-friendly interfaces for searching on Arabic words and their relations targeting Arabic teachers and learners. However, a small minority of dictionaries in general (and none in Arabic to our knowledge) specify the readability level of their words, let alone their lexical relations with other words.

The system we present in this paper exploits a number of developments in Arabic natural language processing (NLP) by different groups of researchers (Black et al., 2006; Graff et al., 2009; Taji et al., 2018; Obeid et al., 2020; Al Khalil et al., 2020) to develop a new online thesaurus that (a) supports different search modes (inflected word, lemma, root and English gloss), (b) provides five types of lexical relations (synonyms, antonyms, hypernyms, hyponyms and related), and (c) indicates the readability level of the word on a five-scale system. This interface allows Arabic speakers and learners to benefit from advances in Arabic NLP technologies. And by exposing these technologies to a large number of users, we expect their feedback will help the researchers who developed the computational and lexical components to identify gaps and errors.

A live link to the demo is available at: `http://samer.camel-lab.com/`.

2 Background and Related Work

In this section, we present the main challenges for processing Arabic, and the various databases and NLP tools we use in developing our system.

Arabic Linguistic Considerations Arabic is a morphologically rich and orthographically ambiguous language. Words have many inflected forms varying in terms of gender, number, person, case, aspect, mood, voice, as well as a large number of attachable clitics, such as pronominal objects and prepositions. Short vowels and consonant doubling are indicated using optional diacritical marks that are mostly elided resulting in a high degree of ambiguity. For example the word فردها *frdhA* has four core lemmas (or

Proceedings of the 27th International Conference on Computational Linguistics, pages 59–63
Barcelona, Spain (Online), December 12, 2020.

lexical abstractions over all inflections): the verbs فَرَّد *far~ad* 'individualize, separate in units', and رَدّ *rad~* 'answer, return'; and the nouns فَرْد *fard* 'individual, unit' and رَدّ *rad~* 'response, return'.[1] The root of the first and third lemmas is [ف.ر.د] *[f.r.d]*, and the root of the other lemmas is [ر.د.د] *[r.d.d]*.

Arabic Natural Language Processing Tools   To address the morphological complexity and orthographic ambiguity, we make use of an open source toolkit for Arabic NLP, Camel Tools (Obeid et al., 2020). We embedded its morphological analyser, CALIMA Star (Taji et al., 2018), in our online system to determine all the lemmas associated with a user's input in word mode. CALIMA Star extends the Standard Arabic Morphological Analyzer (SAMA) (Graff et al., 2009) with a number of additional morphological features. The database covers over 40 thousand lemmas and links each to a part-of-speech (POS), root and English gloss, all of which can be searched on in our interface.

Lexical Modeling with Arabic WordNet   Arabic WordNet (AWN) is a public lexical database of semantic relations between words in Arabic (ElKateb et al., 2006; Black et al., 2006). AWN was developed based on the methods used in EuroWordNet (EWN) (Rodríguez et al., 1998), and is directly mappable to it and to the Princeton Wordnet of English (Fellbaum, 1998). The AWN database currently has 16,066 entries, out of which 5,036 are multi-word phrases. Basic entries are represented as lemmas abstracted from morphological inflections. The AWN entries are organized in 14,284 synonym sets (synsets), some of which are connected through lexical relations such as antonymy, hypernymmy, and others.

The AWN is the *Thesaurus* backbone of our system. We focus on five types of lexical relations: synonym, antonyms, hyponyms, hypernyms and *related*. The first four relations are defined as in AWN. Most other relevant AWN relations are mapped to the *related* relation. In our setup, the synonyms of a lemma x are the union of all the other lemmas in all the synsets containing the lemma x. Similarly, the antonyms of a lemma x are the union of all the lemmas in the synsets that are in an antonym relation with the synsets containing the lemma x.

Arabic Readability   Modeling readability levels is relevant to a range of NLP tasks from developing language education applications to user profiling. Much work has been done on readability leveling and its assessment and specification in English leading to the development of many resources and tools. However, this is not the case for many other languages. A recently developed Arabic Readability Lexicon have filled this gap for Arabic (Al Khalil et al., 2020). Language professionals manually annotated a 26,578-lemma lexicon with a five-level readability scale for MSA targeting native speakers. The levels are as follows: Level I (Grade 1, age 6), Level II (Grade 2-3, age 7-8), Level III (Grade 4-5, age 9-10), Level IV (Grade 6-8, age 11-14), Level V (specialist, age 15 and above).

3 Design and Implementation

We start with a discussion of the design desiderata of our system, followed by details of the database preparation, back-end functionalities and front-end interface.

3.1 Design Specifications

We designed our interface with the following considerations in mind.

- **Handling Arabic Ambiguity and Rich Morphology** The system needs to provide the ability to search on an inflected Arabic word form by relating it to its lemma and POS.
- **Multiple Search Modes** In addition to searching on an inflected word, the system needs to provide the ability to directly search on a lemma with its POS, on an Arabic root, and on an English gloss. Multiword phrases should be also searchable using component words.
- **Rich Lexical and Readability Information** In addition to the readability level of the lemmas associated with the search mode, the system needs to provide lexically related words and phrases.
- **Friendly Navigation** The system needs to allow hyperlink search: the user can click on underlined components of returned search results to explore the network of the used databases.

---

[1] Arabic transliteration is presented in the Habash-Soudi-Buckwalter scheme (Habash et al., 2007).

#	Key	Value	Example
1	lemma#pos	English	سَفَر#noun -> journey, travel, trip
2	lemma#pos	root	كِتاب#noun 'book' -> [ك ت ب]
3	root	(lemma#pos)	[ك ت ب] -> كِتاب#noun 'book', كاتِب#noun 'author'
4	English	(lemma#pos)	book -> كِتاب#noun, سِفَر#noun
5	lemma#pos	readability	كِتاب#noun 'book' -> Level 1
6	lemma#pos	synonyms (lemma#pos)	كِتاب#noun 'book' -> سِفْر#noun 'book'
7	lemma#pos	antonyms (lemma#pos)	اِمْرَأة#noun 'woman -> رَجُل#noun 'man'
8	lemma#pos	hypernyms (lemma#pos)	أَمِير#noun 'prince' -> إِنْسان#noun 'human'
9	lemma#pos	hyponyms (lemma#pos)	إِنْسان#noun 'human' -> أَمِير#noun 'prince'
10	lemma#pos	related expressions (lemma#pos)	أُمّ#noun 'mother' -> دَلَّل#verb 'pamper'
11	lemma#pos	matching phrases (lemma#pos)	بَيْت#noun 'house' -> بيت الشباب#noun 'hostel'

Figure 1: Contents of the Look-up Tables (examples are not complete entries)

3.2 Database Preparation

Our system uses 11 look-up tables to provide the needed support for all the search modes described above. The look-up table key and value information are listed in Figure 1. The primary search key across most of the look-up tables is the lemma and POS concatenated by the hash sign #.

Morphological Look-up Tables Tables 1 through 4 link the lemma#pos to the English gloss and root, and the English gloss and root to lemma#pos. These look-up tables are populated from the Camel Tools databases. The first two provide the specific root and English gloss of a lemma#pos; while the last two link the root and English gloss to *all* the lemma#pos values sharing the same root, or English gloss, respectively. We lower case English words when using them as look-up keys.

Readability Look-up Table Table 5 links the lemma#pos to the readability level. It is populated from the Arabic Readability Lexicon.

Semantic Relation Look-up Tables Tables 6 through 11 link a key lemma#pos to a list of other lemma#pos entries that are in specific semantic relationship to the key lemma#pos. The relation types include synonyms, antonyms, hypernyms, hyponyms, related expressions, and matching phrases (exact lemma#pos match within a larger multiword phrase).

The semantic relation look-up tables are populated from AWN after matching AWN lemmas with Camel Tools lemmas. One challenge we faced is that AWN lemmas and POS are defined slightly differently from Camel Tools, e.g., the lemma for the word 'aroma' is شَذَا#n *šaðaA*#n in AWN but شَذاأ#noun *šaðAā*#noun in Camel Tools. We match the lemmas in an offline process using the MADAMIRA Arabic morphological analyzer and disambiguator (Pasha et al., 2014), which uses the same lemmas and POS as Camel Tools. We run the AWN word and multiword entries through MADAMIRA, and then select the best matches using Levenshtein edit distance, and manual mapping rules between the POS categories.

3.3 Implementation

Our back-end was implemented in Python using Flask.[2] We embedded Camel Tools' Arabic morphological analyzer to process user input Arabic words, and map them to lists of ambiguous lemma#pos entries. These entries are used as keys to look up other features and related lemma#pos entries in the look-up tables. The display of the information includes dynamically creating hyperlinks to search on the lemma#pos, root and English gloss. For the front-end, we used simple JavaScript to control the look and feel of the interface.

---

[2]https://flask.palletsprojects.com/en/1.1.x/

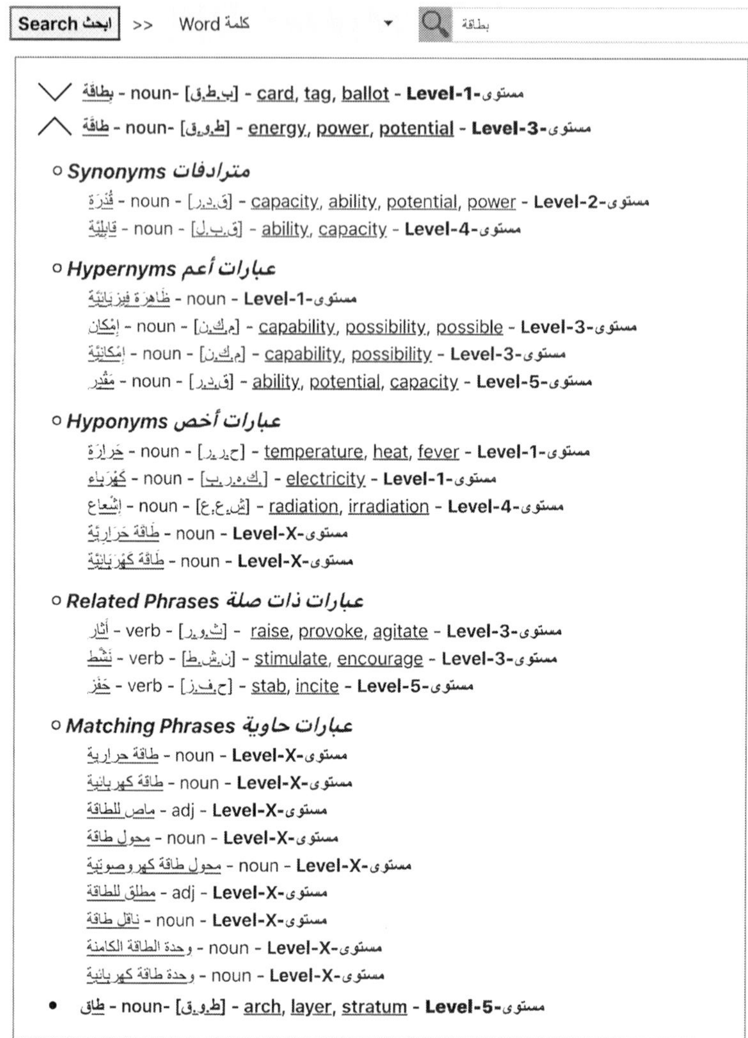

Figure 2: Search Results for the word بطاقة *bTAqħ*

3.4 Example

We illustrate the functionality of our system with the example in Figure 2. For the undiacritized Arabic word بطاقة *bTAqħ* input by a user in Word mode, our server processes the input with the Camel Tools' morphological analyzer generating three analyses: بِطَاقَة#noun *biTaAqaħ* 'ballot', طَاقَة#noun *TaAqaħ* 'energy', and طاق#noun *TaAq* 'arch'. Their English gloss, readability and root details are obtained from look-up tables 1-5 (in Figure 1). These three analyses are shown as the first level result. Once the user clicks on the arrow sign on the side of a first level result, the second level results, or the relations associated with the first level result, are displayed. Those relations' keys (lemma#pos) are obtained from look-up tables 6-11. For each key in those relations, we search look-up tables 1-5 to obtain their English gloss, readability and root information.

4   Conclusion and Future Work

We presented an online readability leveled Arabic thesaurus, created through integrating a number of Arabic NLP tools and data sets. We plan to continue improving on the various elements used in building this interface. The most immediate use of the interface is as part of an effort to simplify Arabic modern novels to younger readers (Al Khalil et al., 2017).

Acknowledgments

This project was supported by a New York University Abu Dhabi Research Enhancement Fund. We would like to thank Salam Khalifa and Ossama Obeid for helpful conversations, and interface design and implementation advice. We thank the anonymous reviewers for their feedback and comments.

References

Muhamed Al Khalil, Nizar Habash, and Hind Saddiki. 2017. Simplification of Arabic masterpieces for extensive reading: A project overview. *Procedia Computer Science*, 117:192–198.

Muhamed Al Khalil, Nizar Habash, and Zhengyang Jiang. 2020. A large-scale leveled readability lexicon for standard Arabic. In *Proceedings of The 12th Language Resources and Evaluation Conference*, pages 3053–3062, Marseille, France, May. European Language Resources Association.

William Black, Sabri Elkateb, Horacio Rodríguez, Musa Alkhalifa, Piek Vossen, Adam Pease, and Christiane Fellbaum. 2006. Introducing the Arabic WordNet project. In *Proceedings of the third international WordNet conference*, pages 295–300. Citeseer.

Sabry ElKateb, William Black, Horacio Rodríguez, Musa Alkhalifa, Piek Vossen, Adam Pease, and Christiane Fellbaum. 2006. Building a WordNet for Arabic. In *Proceedings of the Language Resources and Evaluation Conference (LREC)*, Genoa, Italy.

Christiane Fellbaum. 1998. *WordNet: An Electronic Lexical Database.* MIT Press. http://www.cogsci.princeton.edu/~wn [2000, September 7].

David Graff, Mohamed Maamouri, Basma Bouziri, Sondos Krouna, Seth Kulick, and Tim Buckwalter. 2009. Standard arabic morphological analyzer (sama) version 3.1. *Linguistic Data Consortium LDC2009E73*.

Nizar Habash, Abdelhadi Soudi, and Tim Buckwalter. 2007. On Arabic Transliteration. In A. van den Bosch and A. Soudi, editors, *Arabic Computational Morphology: Knowledge-based and Empirical Methods*, pages 15–22. Springer, Netherlands.

Ossama Obeid, Nasser Zalmout, Salam Khalifa, Dima Taji, Mai Oudah, Bashar Alhafni, Go Inoue, Fadhl Eryani, Alexander Erdmann, and Nizar Habash. 2020. CAMeL tools: An open source python toolkit for Arabic natural language processing. In *Proceedings of The 12th Language Resources and Evaluation Conference*, pages 7022–7032, Marseille, France, May. European Language Resources Association.

Arfath Pasha, Mohamed Al-Badrashiny, Mona T Diab, Ahmed El Kholy, Ramy Eskander, Nizar Habash, Manoj Pooleery, Owen Rambow, and Ryan Roth. 2014. Madamira: A fast, comprehensive tool for morphological analysis and disambiguation of arabic. In *LREC*, volume 14, pages 1094–1101.

Horacio Rodríguez, Salvador Roca, Piek Vossen, Laura Bloksma, Wim Peters, Antonietta Alonge, Francesca Bertagna, and Adriana Roventini. 1998. The top-down strategy for building eurowordnet: Vocabulary coverage, base concepts and top ontology. *Computers and the Humanities*, 32:117–152, 03.

Dima Taji, Salam Khalifa, Ossama Obeid, Fadhl Eryani, and Nizar Habash. 2018. An Arabic morphological analyzer and generator with copious features. In *Proceedings of the Fifteenth Workshop on Computational Research in Phonetics, Phonology, and Morphology*, pages 140–150, Brussels, Belgium, October. Association for Computational Linguistics.

TrainX – Named Entity Linking with Active Sampling and Bi-Encoders

Tom Oberhauser, Tim Bischoff, Karl Brendel, Maluna Menke,
Tobias Klatt, Amy Siu, Felix Alexander Gers, Alexander Löser
Beuth University of Applied Sciences
Berlin, Germany
{toberhauser, tkbischoff, karl.brendel, mmenke,
tobias.klatt, siu, gers, aloeser}@beuth-hochschule.de

Abstract

We demonstrate *TrainX*, a system for Named Entity Linking for medical experts. It combines
state-of-the-art entity recognition and linking architectures, such as Flair and fine-tuned Bi-
Encoders based on BERT, with an easy-to-use interface for healthcare professionals. We support
medical experts in annotating training data by using active sampling strategies to forward infor-
mative samples to the annotator. We demonstrate that our model is capable of linking against
large knowledge bases, such as UMLS (3.6 million entities), and supporting zero-shot cases,
where the linker has never seen the entity before. Those zero-shot capabilities help to mitigate
the problem of rare and expensive training data that is a common issue in the medical domain.

1 Introduction

Named Entity Linking is a well-studied task for decades (Ling et al., 2015). It includes recognizing
and disambiguating mentions of entities in text against a catalogue or a knowledge base. However,
training data is often missing and requires additional expensive labeling, especially in domains like
medicine, where the availability of domain experts for rare diseases is limited. Moreover, novel as well
as uncommon entities such as rare diseases might not have been part of the training data; in that case, the
linker must solve a zero-shot scenario by disambiguating a mention never seen before. Existing easy-
to-use annotation interfaces like prodigy[1] either fail to support entity linking annotations or have limited
support for an end-user to find the correct entity in a large knowledge base. Further, they do not support
the annotator by actively sampling relevant documents to save annotation time. Active-learning-enabled
annotation tools, like INCEpTION (Klie et al., 2018), overcome this problem, but they are optimized
for annotating multiple layers of linguistic features, which makes their user interfaces very complex and
crowded. Using such tools leads to additional training costs for medical professionals.

Contribution   We present *TrainX*, a system that consists of state-of-the-art entity recognition and linking architectures combined with an easy-to-use interface for healthcare professionals. Our system supports medical experts in annotating data and training models for medical named entity linking based on
UMLS (Bodenreider, 2004) with more than 3.6 million entities. By using active sampling, we minimize
labeling efforts. TrainX uses transfer learning by leveraging Bi-Encoders (Gillick et al., 2019; Wu et
al., 2019; Logeswaran et al., 2019; Humeau et al., 2020) for disambiguation and a kNN-index to retrieve candidate entities within milliseconds. We mitigate issues caused by sparse training data by using
zero-shot optimized techniques that can generalize beyond the labels seen in training. To our knowledge,
this is the first named entity linking approach that combines an easy-to-use frontend with the transfer
learning capabilities of recent BERT models. The system is licensed under Apache 2.0 and is available
on GitHub[2].

---

[1] https://prodi.gy/

[2] https://github.com/DATEXIS/TrainX

Proceedings of the 27th International Conference on Computational Linguistics, pages 64–69
Barcelona, Spain (Online), December 12, 2020.

2 Demonstrating Medical Named Entity Linking

In this section, we demonstrate the usage of TrainX for a medical entity linking scenario. Although we show a domain-specific task, TrainX is not limited to the medical domain but can be easily adapted to any entity linking use case with a knowledge base that contains names and short descriptions for every entity. Figure 1 shows the usage of TrainX in an example scenario where existing GOLD annotations are available. First, the annotator begins a new session or resumes an existing one (1). In the case of a new session, she uploads a new dataset (2). After the upload, she obtains sampled documents from the dataset, in order to annotate them (3). The samples view (4) allows her to add new USER annotations (green) or to view/edit GOLD annotations provided in the dataset (yellow). By clicking on an annotation, she can examine details of the linked entity and make a correction if needed by using the annotation helper (5); the modified samples are henceforth USER annotations and marked in green. A full-text search on the UMLS supports the annotator to interactively explore the knowledge base in order to speed up the annotation/examination/correction workflow. By clicking on the checkmark (6), she can mark the entire sample as correct, or she can use the arrows above to request as many further samples as she likes. When one round of annotation is finished, she uploads the annotated samples (7) and starts the training phase (8), while the system will apply the model to the newly adjusted data. She can query the training status at any time (9). When training is finished, she retrieves the newly processed samples (10) and is returned to the samples view, where the predictions of the newly trained model are shown as PRED annotations in blue (11). Now, she can further correct and/or add annotations and iterate the process. A video of this demonstration is available under https://youtu.be/XAt94UNEEQ4.

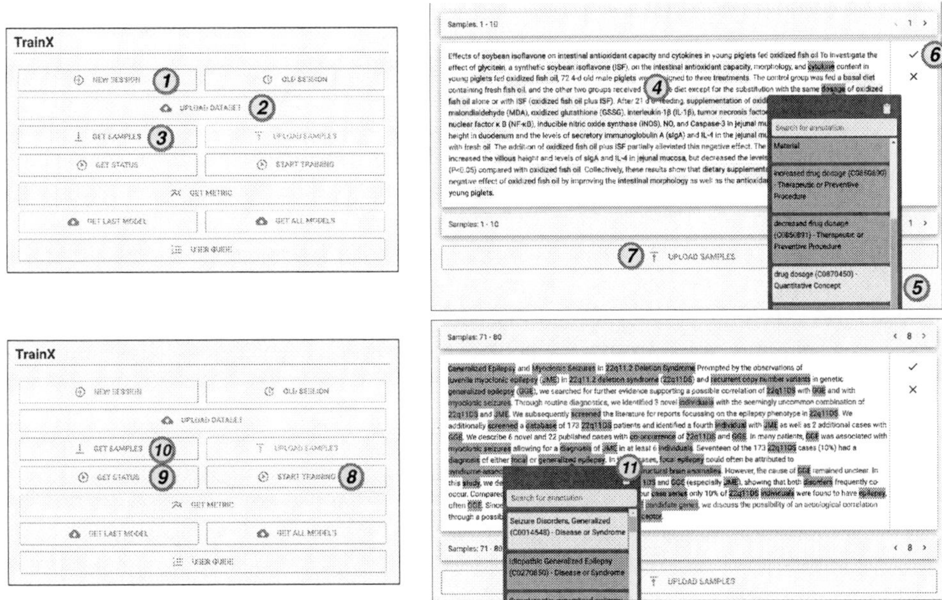

Figure 1: Usage of the TrainX system to train and evaluate the entity linker on a mixture of given GOLD and added USER labels. The screenshots show the menu, where a user requests samples or starts the training and the sample view where she can edit annotations.

3 Named Entity Linking with Active Sampling and Bi-Encoders

A system component overview is shown in Figure 2. Prior to training, the system needs to be initialized with the knowledge base (UMLS in our case) and an optional set of pre-training documents (1). After the initialization, the user can upload her documents (2) and annotate (3) them using the support of the annotation helper (4). The user is supported by an active sampling of further samples to annotate and correct. Next, the updated annotations and the current model are sent to training component where the named entity recognizer and linker are now (re-)trained on the supplied data (5). After the training succeeded, the newly trained model is used to recognize and link mentions in the uploaded documents to provide feedback to the user (6).

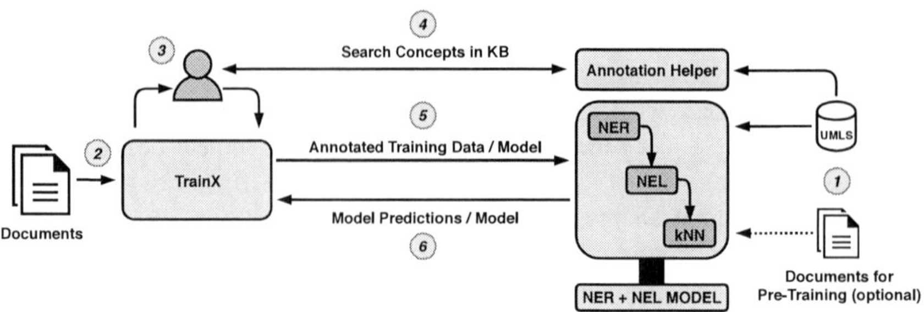

Figure 2: Workflow of the TrainX system.

Named Entity Recognition and Linking with Bi-Encoders The recognition step is the first step of an entity-linking pipeline. A high recall is crucial because the linker will not be able to disambiguate mentions that have not been found by the recognizer in the first place. We chose the Flair-framework (Akbik et al., 2018) because it has proven to achieve state-of-the-art results (Devlin et al., 2018). We implemented a Bi-Encoder based on the work by Wu et al. (2019) and Humeau et al. (2020). The Bi-Encoder uses fine-tuned BERT models to project mentions and entities in a common dense vector space to allow retrieval based on vector similarity. The projection is enforced using a cross-entropy loss function on both encoders' output that rewards a high similarity between the mention and the matching entity representation. In contrast to other entity linking architectures such as the entity linker from the "ScispaCy" framework (Neumann et al., 2019), the Bi-Encoder approach is fully focused on solving zero-shot problems (Wu et al., 2019). Also, it allows us to apply confidence measurements needed for our active sampling mechanisms. We chose not to implement an additional cross-encoder as proposed by Wu et al. (2019), Logeswaran et al. (2019) and Humeau et al. (2020) due to computational efficiency (Kurz et al., 2020). The Bi-Encoder consists a mention encoder $y_m = (pool(T_1(m))$ and an entity encoder $y_e = (pool(T_2(e))$. T_1 and T_2 are BERT models, and m and e are sequences of WordPiece tokens that encode mention and entity, respectively. The pooling method $pool()$ aggregates the resulting tensor into single vector representations y_m and y_e by using the vector of the [CLS] token as a representation of the whole token sequence.

Training the Bi-Encoder Our system works with three types of labels: GOLD for labels from (optional) pre-training data, USER labels that have been created or updated by the user, and PRED labels that were predicted from the entity linker. We train on GOLD and USER labels. For the mention encoder T_1, the mention and its context are encoded by using two special tokens to mark the beginning and end of a mention i.e. `[CLS] context_left [MS] mention [ME] context_right [SEP]`. The input of the entity encoder T_2 is the name of the entity, followed by a textual description, i.e. `[CLS] name [ENT] description [SEP]`. The description for every entity is generated by concatenation of all English descriptions within the UMLS for that concept, starting with the longest one. The maximum number of WordPiece tokens is a hyper-parameter of the model (Wu et al., 2019). Following Humeau et al. (2020), we fine-tune all BERT layers except the embeddings to minimize the cross-entropy loss for a vector of the logits $y_{m_i} \cdot y_{e_1}, \ldots, y_{m_i} \cdot y_{e_i}, \ldots, y_{m_i} \cdot y_{e_n}$ for every (m_i, e_i) in the batch B where $|B| = n$.

Candidate Retrieval For a given mention embedding, the system retrieves an entity by performing a kNN-search based on a normalized dot product between that embedding and all of the concept embeddings. Because an exact kNN search will be too slow in practice for large amounts of data, we will not only examine retrieval performance based on exact kNN, but also on an approximate kNN approach, namely "Hierarchical Navigable Small World graphs" (HNSW) (Malkov and Yashunin, 2020) using the implementation of Facebook AI Similarity Search (Faiss) (Johnson et al., 2017). HNSW outperforms other approximate kNN approaches in terms of quality/speed trade-off (Aumüller et al., 2017).

Hyperparameters Our Bi-Encoder fine-tunes BERT-base models with a learning rate of 5-e5, as suggested by Devlin et al. (2018). As further hyperparameters, we chose a maximum input length of 50 WordPiece tokens for both encoders, a batch size of 128 samples and 100 learning-rate warmup steps. The HNSW indexes are initialized with $m = 16$, $efConstruction = 100$ and $efSearch = 100$.

Active Sampling The goal of our human-in-the-loop process is two-fold: First, the user should become familiar with the quality of the model and second, the system should support the user to improve the performance of the model quickly. The system applies the model to the data after the training and enables the user to approve or correct results. Thereby it selects samples based on the confidence of the named entity recognizer and named entity linker. For each annotation, we calculate the confidence $conf_{ann}$ by aggregating the confidence of the NER $conf_{NER}(ann)$, as provided by the Flair framework, and the confidence of the entity linker based on margin sampling (Scheffer et al., 2001) by taking into account the difference between the retrieved candidate entities at first and second places (e_{ann_1}, e_{ann_2}) with respect to the query vector $q = T_1(ann)$: $conf_{ann} = conf_{NER}(ann) + (cos(q, e_{ann_1}) - cos(q, e_{ann_2}))$. The documents are sampled based on their least confident annotations.

4   Evaluation and Discussion

Evaluation on MedMentions We chose the publicly available "MedMentions-ST21pv" dataset (Mohan and Li, 2019) containing 4,392 annotated abstracts of PubMed articles with 203,282 annotations of 25,419 unique concepts. We use the pre-defined train/test/dev split. The test set contains annotations for 3,590 concepts that have not been in the training set which allows us to evaluate zero-shot capabilities. As named entity recognizer, we selected the Flair framework (Akbik et al., 2018) and trained it on BIOES tagging until the early-stop mechanism of Flair stopped the training process. The scores of this model resulted in a precision of 69.2, a recall of 69.0 and an F1 of 69.1. In Table 1, we report the retrieval scores of the isolated entity linking component in comparison to a BM25-based Elasticsearch[3] full-text index baseline. Table 1 also provides an end-to-end evaluation of the whole pipeline using the micro-averaged A2W weak annotation match metric proposed by Cornolti et al. (2013).

| | UMLS concepts $\in$ MedMentions | | | | | full English UMLS | | | | |
| | full test set | | | only zero-shot | | full test set | | | only zero-shot | |
	BM25	exact	HNSW	exact	HNSW	BM25	exact	HNSW	exact	HNSW
R@1	40.9	63.2	63.2	50.3	50.0	21.7	44.4	43.4	26.5	25.3
R@20	73.7	86.2	86.1	76.3	76.0	50.7	73.6	71.7	55.6	53.1
	End-to-End (NER + NEL)									
Precision	-	47.4	47.4	-	-	-	32.1	31.1	-	-
Recall	-	45.7	45.7	-	-	-	30.9	30.0	-	-
F1	-	46.5	46.5	-	-	-	31.5	30.6	-	-

Table 1: Retrieval Performance – The upper half shows the the recall@k performance of the entity linker compared to the BM25 baseline for exact kNN and HNSW indexes of all the UMLS concepts that can be found within the MedMentions dataset (25,419) or the full English UMLS (3.6 Million). A separate zero-shot evaluation shows the performance of the linker on concepts that it has not seen during training. The lower half provides an end-to-end evaluation of the whole pipeline.

Discussion The Bi-Encoder outperforms the BM25 based approach by a margin of more than 20 percentage points. With respect to the size of the concept database of 3.6 million concepts and given that UMLS still contains many ambiguities (Shooshan et al., 2009), the Bi-Encoder is still able to link to the correct concept 26.5 percent of the times even though it has never seen it during training (zero-shot). On the full test set, which contains a mixture of seen data and zero-shot, the Bi-Encoder was able to link to

---

[3]https://www.elastic.co/

the exact entity in 44.4% of all cases. HNSW reduces the retrieval performance about one percentage point at worse but speeds up the query process to 3ms instead of 600ms per query. The inclusion of the named entity recognizer reduces the recall to 30.9% and results in an overall F1 score 31.5% for exact kNN and 30.6% for HNSW. The zero-shot performance indicates that the underlying Bi-Encoder is able to generalize beyond concepts seen in training to mitigate problems caused by sparse training data. Therefore, our further work will focus on the optimization of the Bi-Encoder and the named entity recognition step in order to better adapt to sparse-training data situations.

Acknowledgements

Our work is funded by the German Federal Ministry for Economic Affairs and Energy (BMWi) under grant agreement 01MK20008D (Service-Meister).

References

Alan Akbik, Duncan Blythe, and Roland Vollgraf. 2018. Contextual String Embeddings for Sequence Labeling. In *COLING 2018, 27th International Conference on Computational Linguistics*, pages 1638–1649.

Martin Aumüller, Erik Bernhardsson, and Alexander Faithfull. 2017. ANN-Benchmarks: A Benchmarking Tool for Approximate Nearest Neighbor Algorithms. In *International Conference on Similarity Search and Applications*, pages 34–49. Springer.

Olivier Bodenreider. 2004. The Unified Medical Language System (UMLS): integrating biomedical terminology. *Nucleic acids research*, 32(suppl_1):D267–D270.

Marco Cornolti, Paolo Ferragina, and Massimiliano Ciaramita. 2013. A Framework for Benchmarking Entity-Annotation Systems. In *Proceedings of the 22nd International Conference on World Wide Web*, WWW '13, page 249–260, New York, NY, USA. Association for Computing Machinery.

Jacob Devlin, Ming-Wei Chang, Kenton Lee, and Kristina Toutanova. 2018. BERT: Pre-training of Deep Bidirectional Transformers for Language Understanding. *arXiv preprint arXiv:1810.04805*.

Daniel Gillick, Sayali Kulkarni, Larry Lansing, Alessandro Presta, Jason Baldridge, Eugene Ie, and Diego Garcia-Olano. 2019. Learning Dense Representations for Entity Retrieval. *arXiv preprint arXiv:1909.10506*.

Samuel Humeau, Kurt Shuster, Marie-Anne Lachaux, and Jason Weston. 2020. Poly-encoders: Architectures and Pre-training Strategies for Fast and Accurate Multi-sentence Scoring. In *8th International Conference on Learning Representations, ICLR*.

Jeff Johnson, Matthijs Douze, and Hervé Jégou. 2017. Billion-scale similarity search with GPUs. *arXiv preprint arXiv:1702.08734*.

Jan-Christoph Klie, Michael Bugert, Beto Boullosa, Richard Eckart de Castilho, and Iryna Gurevych. 2018. The INCEpTION Platform: Machine-Assisted and Knowledge-Oriented Interactive Annotation. In Dongyan Zhao, editor, *COLING 2018, The 27th International Conference on Computational Linguistics: System Demonstrations, Santa Fe, New Mexico, August 20-26, 2018*, pages 5–9. Association for Computational Linguistics.

Nadja Kurz, Felix Hamann, and Adrian Ulges. 2020. Neural Entity Linking on Technical Service Tickets. *arXiv preprint arXiv:2005.07604*.

Xiao Ling, Sameer Singh, and Daniel S Weld. 2015. Design Challenges for Entity Linking. *Transactions of the Association for Computational Linguistics*, 3:315–328.

Lajanugen Logeswaran, Ming-Wei Chang, Kenton Lee, Kristina Toutanova, Jacob Devlin, and Honglak Lee. 2019. Zero-Shot Entity Linking by Reading Entity Descriptions. In *Proceedings of the 57th Annual Meeting of the Association for Computational Linguistics*, pages 3449–3460.

Yu A. Malkov and D. A. Yashunin. 2020. Efficient and Robust Approximate Nearest Neighbor Search Using Hierarchical Navigable Small World Graphs. *IEEE Transactions on Pattern Analysis and Machine Intelligence*, 42(4):824–836, Apr.

Sunil Mohan and Donghui Li. 2019. MedMentions: A Large Biomedical Corpus Annotated with UMLS Concepts. In *Automated Knowledge Base Construction (AKBC)*.

Mark Neumann, Daniel King, Iz Beltagy, and Waleed Ammar. 2019. ScispaCy: Fast and Robust Models for Biomedical Natural Language Processing. In *Proceedings of the 18th BioNLP Workshop and Shared Task*, pages 319–327, Florence, Italy, August. Association for Computational Linguistics.

Tobias Scheffer, Christian Decomain, and Stefan Wrobel. 2001. Active Hidden Markov Models for Information Extraction. In *Proceedings of the 4th International Conference on Advances in Intelligent Data Analysis*, IDA '01, page 309–318, Berlin, Heidelberg. Springer-Verlag.

Sonya E Shooshan, James G Mork, and A Aronson. 2009. Ambiguity in the UMLS Metathesaurus. In *Tech rep, US National Library of Medicine*.

Ledell Wu, Fabio Petroni, Martin Josifoski, Sebastian Riedel, and Luke Zettlemoyer. 2019. Zero-shot Entity Linking with Dense Entity Retrieval. *arXiv preprint arXiv:1911.03814*.

BullStop: A Mobile App for Cyberbullying Prevention

Semiu Salawu
Aston University
Birmingham, B4 7ET
United Kingdom
salawusd@aston.ac.uk

Yulan He
University of Warwick
Coventry, CV4 7AL
United Kingdom
yulan.he@warwick.ac.uk

Jo Lumsden
Aston University
Birmingham, B4 7ET
United Kingdom
lumsdenj@aston.ac.uk

Abstract

Social media has become the new playground for bullies. Young people are now regularly exposed to a wide range of abuse online. In response to the increasing prevalence of cyberbullying, online social networks have increased efforts to clamp down on online abuse but unfortunately, the nature, complexity and sheer volume of cyberbullying means that many cyberbullying incidents go undetected. BullStop is a mobile app for detecting and preventing cyberbullying and online abuse on social media platforms. It uses deep learning models to identify instances of cyberbullying and can automatically initiate actions such as deleting offensive messages and blocking bullies on behalf of the user. Our system not only achieves impressive prediction results but also demonstrates excellent potential for use in real-world scenarios and is freely available on the Google Play Store.

1 Introduction

Cyberbullying is defined as 'wilful and repeated harm inflicted through the use of computers, cell phones, and other electronic devices (Hinduja and Patchin, 2006, pg. 152). It is estimated that as many as 59% of US teenagers would have experienced some form of cyberbullying by the time they become young adults (Pew Research Center, 2018). Nowhere is cyberbullying more prevalent than on social media, where, as much as 69% of reported incidents of cyberbullying took place (Ofcom Research, 2019). In response to the increased proliferation of online abuse, social media platforms like Twitter, Facebook, and Instagram have, in recent years, introduced policies and features to combat and mitigant cyberbullying and its effects. These include preventing the creation of multiple accounts using similar details and suspending abusive users. Human moderators are also employed by online social networks to review thousands of posts daily. Unfortunately, such is the prevalence of cyberbullying, and online harassment that, despite these efforts, it remains a significant online risk for many young people. Furthermore, as cyberbullying is highly subjective, what is deemed offensive differs amongst people, human moderators can only apply generalised rules in making a judgement.

Existing mobile tools to combat cyberbullying mostly either use wordlists or lack the flexibility to cope with the evolving nature of social media. Lempa *et al.* (2015) developed a "sentence checker" mobile app that allows users to check for offensive content in messages before sending. However, as the app is incapable of sending messages or integrating with other messaging applications, users will have to type or copy the message to other messaging applications to send the message. Vishwamitra *et al.* (2017) developed MCDefender, a mobile app that serves as a cyberbullying detection companion to the Facebook app. The app detects words typed in the Facebook app and analyses each word to determine if the user is engaging in bullying activities. The app's tight integration to the Facebook app, however, exposes some limitations. For example, the app cannot detect messages sent if Facebook is accessed via a web browser or if an unofficial Facebook messaging app is used. A better implementation would be to integrate via the social media platform's API, which is the approach adopted by our system.

Proceedings of the 27th International Conference on Computational Linguistics, pages 70–74
Barcelona, Spain (Online), December 12, 2020.

There are two critical challenges in developing viable tools to combat cyberbullying on social media. These are; the evolution of the mainly colloquial language used in social media and the need for the tool to react in a timely fashion to cope with real-time communication. To overcome these challenges, our system uses a microservices-based architecture that allows the introduction of classifiers in a "plug and play" manner and leverages containerisation and cloud-based technologies to exponentially scale to meet the demands of a modern social media platform. In this paper, we present BullStop; a mobile app developed to help young people combat cyberbullying and online abuse. While Twitter is currently supported, it is designed to work with multiple social media platforms.

2 Architecture

The app utilises a novel approach comprised of two key strategies. Firstly, the detection of cyberbullying and online abuse is modelled on how email applications treat spam. It uses a generalised deep learning model to identify the majority of cyberbullying instances and then improves the base model via online training utilising the user's input as ground truth. In this way, the app becomes a personalised cyberbullying detector for each user with a deep understanding of how the user communicates. Secondly, the use of a loosely coupled microservices architecture disassociates the deep learning model from the rest of the system, thus allowing models to be "plug and play". Thus, any model can be easily incorporated into the system; all that is required is a model capable of multi-label classification that accepts textual data and provides its output in the required JSON format. This dramatically improves the system's flexibility, allowing newer and more advanced classifiers to be introduced into the system as required.

The system architecture is illustrated in Figure 1. Messages and contact information from the online social network are introduced into the system via the Synchroniser or Webhook. The Synchroniser is a mobile component that performs regular data harmonisation with online social networks. It connects to the social media platform via an API and extracts new messages, posts and contacts from the user's account. The Webhook provides a similar function, but unlike the Synchroniser which retrieves information on a schedule via a pull mechanism, the Webhook receives new data via a push from the online social network. The Webhook is an optional component only used when the social media platform provides a mechanism to send such notifications. It is an event-triggered feature that allows the social network to send new data to an external interface when monitored events occur, for example, a new friend request or message received. Data received from the online social network is placed on the Message Queue where it is processed by the Abuse Detection Module (ADM).

The ADM is comprised of one or more machine learning models that predict the labels for the messages retrieved from the Message Queue. The models have been trained to predict the labels, *Cyberbullying, Insult, Profanity, Sarcasm, Threat, Exclusion, Spa, Porn* for each message. BERT, DistilBERT, RoBERTA and XLNET are some of the models available in the ADM, but other models can be easily added. The labels predicted for a message can be corrected by the user, and these are stored and used to retrain the model. The output from the ADM determines actions taken by the Marshaller. The Marshaller communicates with the social networks via the API and initiates appropriate actions on behalf of the user.

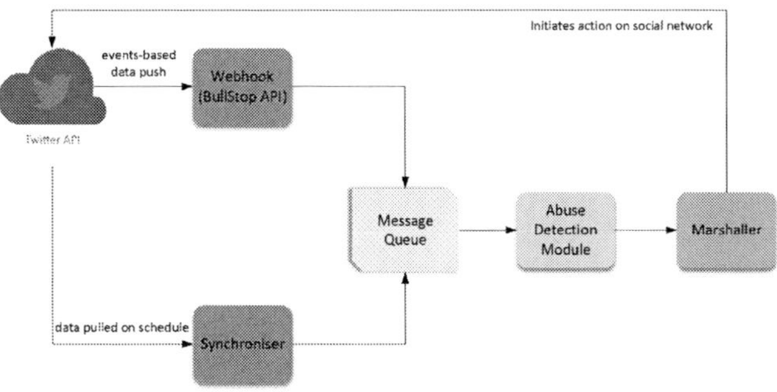

Figure 1: High Level Architecture.

3   Use Case

UI design is a critical component for mobile apps, more so for the young target audience of our system. Therefore, from the onset, the app was designed to appeal to this audience, and many of the design decisions taken were in furtherance of this goal. Feedback from a cross-section of stakeholders, including young people, parents, educators, law enforcement and child mental health professionals was actively sought and influenced the user interface of the application. For the adult stakeholders, we conducted six focus group sessions to gain insight into their views on cyberbullying and its prevention. Individual interviews were then conducted with twenty-five adolescents representing the target audience which was followed by a participatory design phase where six young people worked with us to collaboratively design the mobile application. The functionalities and UI of the mobile app is based on the outcome of these sessions.

After installing the app, users are prompted to create a profile which is used to store their settings and preferences. Industry-standard cryptographic and encryption technologies are used to create and manage accounts securely. Users can then associate their profiles with social network accounts (see Figure 2) and configure personal settings (see Figure 3). The app will continuously monitor the associated social media accounts for new messages/posts to analyse. Relevant labels are assigned to the message based on the model's prediction (see Figure 4). Each label is associated with a score, and the cumulative score for the message is computed and compared against the user's preferences which determine if the message should be deleted and the sender blocked. Users can review received messages (including deleted ones) and update the assigned labels. Any such message is used by the app as data for online training. We acknowledged that providing users with the ability to read deleted offensive messages in order to re-classify them may seem counterproductive. The stakeholders were however in favour of this feature, and as a mitigating feature, the app permanently removes the most offensive messages automatically after a configurable period.

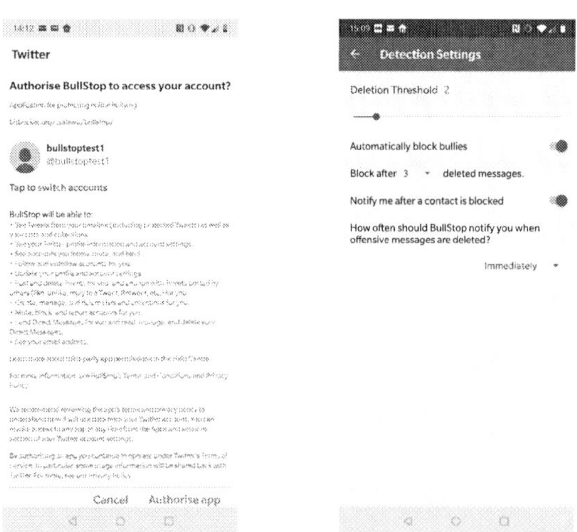
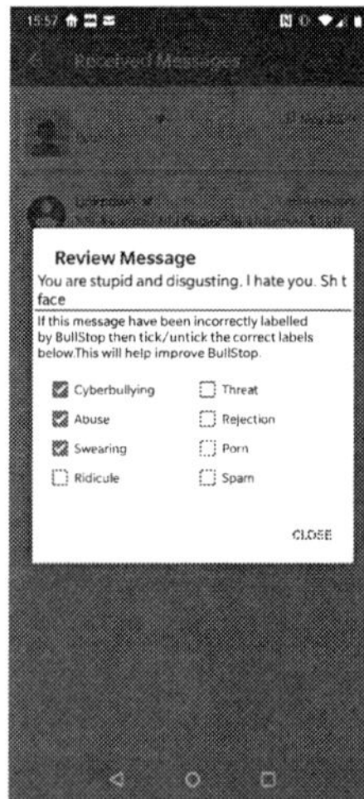

Figure 2: Authorisation Screen   Figure 3: Settings Screen   Figure 4: Message Screen

4   Experiments

Dataset. The models used in the ADM were trained on 62,587 tweets extracted from Twitter using query terms designed to return offensive tweets. Query terms used included the 15 most frequently used profane words on Twitter (Wang *et al.*, 2014) as well as hashtags such as #sarcasm, #stayinyourlane, #maga, #blacklivesmatter to capture different forms of online abuse and bullying. Our collection strategy was aimed at creating a dataset with high concentration of bullying content. This approach differs from standard practice, which seeks to emulate natural distribution and typically results in datasets with minimal cyberbullying content thus requiring oversampling techniques to improve cyberbullying distribution within the dataset. We used a pool of 17 annotators to label the dataset, and each annotator was provided with 6,000 – 10,000 tweets. Each tweet was assigned to 3 different annotators and majority agreement required for each label. Krippendorff's Alpha (rater agreement) was calculated to be 0.67. Standard preprocessing steps including removal of punctuation, symbols, non-ASCII characters, user mentions, URL and lower casing were performed. The number of tweets associated with each class is as shown in Table 1.

Label	Profanity	Porn	Insult	Spam	Bullying	Sarcasm	Threat	Exclusion	None
Count	51,014	16,690	15,201	14,827	3,254	117	79	10	10,768

Table 1: Total number of tweets each label was assigned to.

Evaluation. We trained a set of traditional classifiers (Multinomial Naive Bayes, Linear SVC, Logistic Regression) and deep learning-based models (BERT, RoBERTa, XLNet, DistilBERT) on the dataset. BERT (Bidirectional Encoder Representations from Transformers) is a language representation model used to pre-train deep bi-directional representations from unlabeled text (Devlin *et al.*, 2018). RoBERTa (Robustly Optimized BERT Pretraining Approach) is an optimised BERT-based model (Liu *et al.*, 2019) trained using ten times more data than BERT to improve performance. DistilBERT (Distilled BERT) is a compacted BERT-based model (Sanh *et al.*, 2019) that requires fewer computing resources and training time than BERT but preserves most of BERT performance gains with little performance degradation. XLNet (Yang *et al.*, 2019) is an autoregressive BERT-like model designed to overcome some of the limitations of BERT. We utilised both pre-trained versions of the deep learning models as well as fine-tuning the models on our dataset. The deep learning models outperformed the baseline classifiers with Multinomial Naive Bayes emerging as the worst classifier across the experiments (see Table 2). An interesting discovery was also that the pre-trained models performed better than the fine-tuned models, which is in agreement with the findings of Radiya-Dixit and Wang (2020). A probable reason for this is because our dataset is much smaller than the corpus used for pre-training and as such, the models were unable to learn additional context during fine-tuning. The overall best classifier was RoBERTa using pre-trained weights. Consequently, this was the model used in our system.

Model	Macro ROC-AUC($\uparrow$)	Accuracy ($\uparrow$)	Hamming Loss ($\downarrow$)	Macro $F_1(\uparrow$)	Micro $F_1(\uparrow$)
Multinomial Naive Bayes	0.8030	0.4568	0.1014	0.2618	0.7200
Linear SVC	0.8353	0.5702	0.0866	0.3811	0.7674
Logistic Regression	0.8354	0.5743	0.0836	0.3587	0.7725
BERT (pre-trained)	0.9657	0.5817	0.0736	**0.6318**	0.7998
DistilBERT (pre-trained)	0.9675	0.5802	0.0764	0.5202	0.7855
RoBERTa (pre-trained)	**0.9695**	0.5785	**0.0722**	0.5437	**0.8081**
XLNet(pre-trained)	0.9679	0.5806	0.0738	0.5441	0.8029
BERT (fine-trained)	0.9651	0.5822	0.0725	0.5300	0.8022
DistilBERT (fine-trained)	0.9633	**0.5834**	0.0753	0.5040	0.7872
RoBERTa (fine-trained)	0.9670	0.5794	0.0724	0.5329	0.8044
XLNet(fine-trained)	0.9654	0.5819	0.0741	0.5308	0.8037

Table 2: Results of classification. ($\uparrow$: higher the better; $\downarrow$: lower the better)

5   Conclusion

We have presented our system for fine-grained detection and prevention of cyberbullying and online abuse on social media. Besides its flexible architecture which allows the use of any classifier, it incorporates online training using ground truth provided by the user for retraining. The app is available on the Google Play Store (https://play.google.com/store/apps/details?id=mobile.bullstop.io), and future work planned includes the use of multiple classifiers and the expansion of the original dataset to include more tweets and content from other online social networks.

References

Evani, Radiya-Dixit and Xin Wang. 2020. How fine can fine-tuning be? Learning efficient language models. *Computing Research Repository*, arXiv:2004.14129. Version 1.

Jacob Devlin and Ming-Wei Chang and Kenton Lee and Kristina Toutanova. 2018. BERT: Pre-training of Deep Bidirectional Transformers for Language Understanding. *Computing Research Repository*, arXiv:1810.04805. Version 2.

Justin W. Patchin and Sameer Hinduja. 2006. Bullies Move Beyond the Schoolyard. *Youth Violence and Juvenile Justice*, 4(2):148–169

Nishant Vishwamitra, Xiang Zhang, Jonathan Tong, Hongxin Hu, Feng Luo, Robin Kowalski, and Joseph Mazer. 2017. MCDefender: Toward effective cyberbullying defense in mobile online social networks. In Proceedings of the 3rd ACM International Workshop on Security and Privacy Analytics 2017, pages 37-42, Arizona, USA.

Ofcom Research. 2019. Online Nation. [online] ofcom.org.uk. Available at: `https://www.ofcom.org.uk/__data/assets/pdf_file/0025/149146/online-nation-report.pdf`

Pawel Lempa, Michal Ptaszynski and Fumito Masui. 2015. Cyberbullying Blocker Application for Android. In Proceedings of the 7th Language & Technology Conference 2015, pages 408 - 412, Poznan, Poland.

Pew Research Center. 2018. A Majority of Teens Have Experienced Some Form of Cyberbullying. [online] pewresearch.org. Available at: `https://www.pewresearch.org/internet/wp-content/uploads/sites/9/2018/09/PI_2018.09.27_teens-and-cyberbullying_FINAL.pdf`

Victor Sanh, Lysandre Debut, Julien Chaumond, and Thomas Wolf. 2019. DistilBERT, a distilled version of BERT: smaller, faster, cheaper and lighter. *Computing Research Repository*, arXiv:1910.01108. Version 4.

Wenbo Wang, Lu Chen, Krishnaprasad Thirunarayan, and Amit P. Sheth. 2014. Cursing in English on Twitter. In Proceedings of the 17th ACM conference on Computer supported cooperative work social computing, pages 415-425, Baltimore, USA.

Yinhan Liu, Myle Ott, Naman Goyal, Jingfei Du, Mandar Joshi, Danqi Chen, Omer Levy, Mike Lewis, Luke Zettlemoyer and Veselin Stoyanov. 2019. RoBERTa: A Robustly Optimized BERT Pretraining Approach. *Computing Research Repository*, arXiv:1907.11692 Version 1.

Yu D. Weider, Maithili Gole, Nishanth Prabhuswamy, Sowmya Prakash, and Vidya Gowdru Shankaramurthy. 2016. An approach to design and analyze the framework for preventing cyberbullying. In Proceedings of IEEE International Conference on Services Computing, 2016, pages 864-867, San Francisco, USA.

Zhilin Yang, Zihang Dai, Yiming Yang, Jaime Carbonell, Russ R. Salakhutdinov, and Quoc V. Le. 2019. XLNet: Generalized Autoregressive Pretraining for Language Understanding. *Computing Research Repository*, arXiv:1906.08237 Version 2.

Annobot: Platform for Annotating and Creating Datasets through Conversation with a Chatbot

Rafał Poświata and Michał Perełkiewicz
National Information Processing Institute
al. Niepodległości 188b, 00-608 Warsaw, Poland
{rposwiata, mperelkiewicz}@opi.org.pl

Abstract

In this paper, we introduce Annobot: a platform for annotating and creating datasets through conversation with a chatbot. This natural form of interaction has allowed us to create a more accessible and flexible interface, especially for mobile devices. Our solution has a wide range of applications such as data labelling for binary, multi-class/label classification tasks, preparing data for regression problems, or creating sets for issues such as machine translation, question answering or text summarization. Additional features include pre-annotation, active sampling, online learning and real-time inter-annotator agreement. The system is integrated with the popular messaging platform: Facebook Messanger. Usability experiment showed the advantages of the proposed platform compared to other labelling tools. The source code of Annobot is available under the GNU LGPL license at https://github.com/rafalposwiata/annobot.

1 Introduction

The basis of any machine learning model is data. In the case of supervised solutions, such data must be labelled, very often manually, especially if problems are closely related to human interpretation such as emotion classification (Mohammad et al., 2018) or hate/offensive language detection (Zampieri et al., 2019). The preparation of such data sets is most often carried out using the crowdsourcing platforms such as Figure Eight (earlier called CrowdFlower)[1] or Amazon Mechanical Turk[2]. These platforms undoubtedly have many advantages, but they are paid solutions that not everyone can afford. Furthermore, due to their commercial nature, no changes or modifications can be made on your own. There are also open-source solutions on the market, but you have to organize a group of labellers yourself. Another labelling issue is the lack of an intuitive, flexible, well-known, and responsive user interface. Taking into account the above and the fact that chatbot technology has recently become more widespread, we decided to create the Annobot platform. This is the first open-sourced platform for annotating and creating datasets through conversation with a chatbot. This natural form of interaction provides an interface that meets all criteria, while integration with the messaging application allows for more efficient activation of users.

The rest of the paper is organized as follows. Section 2 briefly describes open-source text annotation systems developed so far. Section 3 shows an overview of our platform and its detail functions. Experiment for showing the effectiveness of the created system is presented in Section 4. Next section presents possible applications and impact. Finally, Section 6 concludes this paper.

---

[1]https://www.figure-eight.com/
[2]https://www.mturk.com/

Proceedings of the 27th International Conference on Computational Linguistics, pages 75–79
Barcelona, Spain (Online), December 12, 2020.

2   Related Work

If we trace the history of labelling tools[3], most of them have been created for sequence tagging (Stenetorp et al., 2012; Yimam et al., 2013; Bontcheva et al., 2013; Yang et al., 2018;
Kummerfeld, 2019; Lin et al., 2019). Recent years have brought tools for other purposes such
as annotating dialogues (Collins et al., 2019), documents (Nakayama et al., 2018), and other
types of data (Heartex, 2019). When considering the user interface, most tools offer GUI (all
mentioned before), although there are also alternative approaches such as command line (Yang
et al., 2018; Kummerfeld, 2019). What's worth mentioning is that the latest tools claim to
support mobile versions (Nakayama et al., 2018; Lin et al., 2019; Heartex, 2019) and have more
and more innovative functionalities, here we can mention AlpacaTag, which has, e.g. active,
intelligent recommendations or automatic crowd consolidation module. Our solution is in line
with current trends related to support for mobile devices and advanced additional functionalities
(e.g. active sampling). However, we have applied a different form of interaction than in other
tools, namely CUI (Conversational User Interface). Our tool is integrated with a platform with
billions of users (Facebook) and has a very wide list of possible applications resulting from the
CUI.

3   Platform Overview

As shown in Figure 1, the Annobot platform consists of five modules. **Annobot
chat** and **Facebook Messenger** are ded-
icated to users/labellers, while **Annobot
admin panel** is used to manage the platform (including adding data sets or preparing a conversation scenario). These are
web-based components. The main module
is the **Annobot core**. It is a server application, responsible for receiving, sending,
and recording all operations performed
within the platform and integrating it with
Facebook. The **ML models** module is a
set of machine learning models used for
more advance functions described later on.

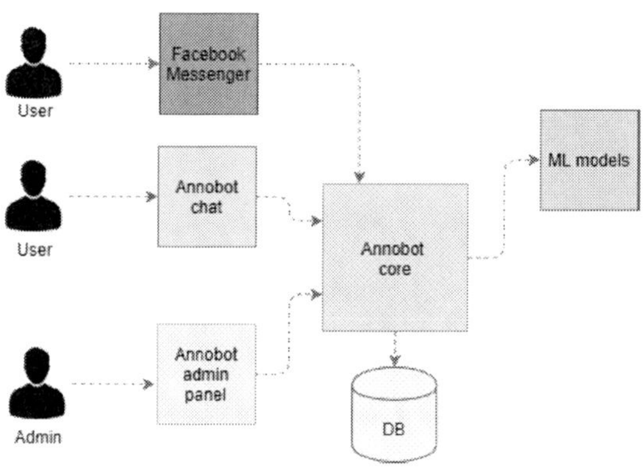

Figure 1: Overview of the Annobot platform.

3.1   Functionalities

Annotating through conversation is the main functionality of our platform. To make a chatbot
available to people, you must first configure it. We start by naming the bot and, if we want to
use advanced features, adding the URL to the ml models. Then we can integrate our bot with
Facebook. Next, you need to create a conversation schema. The schema is our planned scenario,
according to which the bot works. It consists of any number of steps, belonging to one of four
classes: simple message, question, sample for labelling or model prediction. In Figure 2a there
is an example of such a configuration. In this example, the first two steps are a simple welcome
message and the question about age. The third step corresponds to the actual labelling data.
The administrator has to specify the data set, user input type (e.g. label), the labelling scheme
(e.g., binary), possible labels (e.g., positive/negative), and instructions for the labellers. The
last step allows you to test the chatbot (exactly saying the selected model - SVM_binary), to
which the user can send his text. Examples of conversations between a labeller and a chatbot
created according to this scheme is shown in Figure 2b. In addition to this functionality, the
system also has other features, which we will present below.

---

[3]We only considered non-commercial tools.

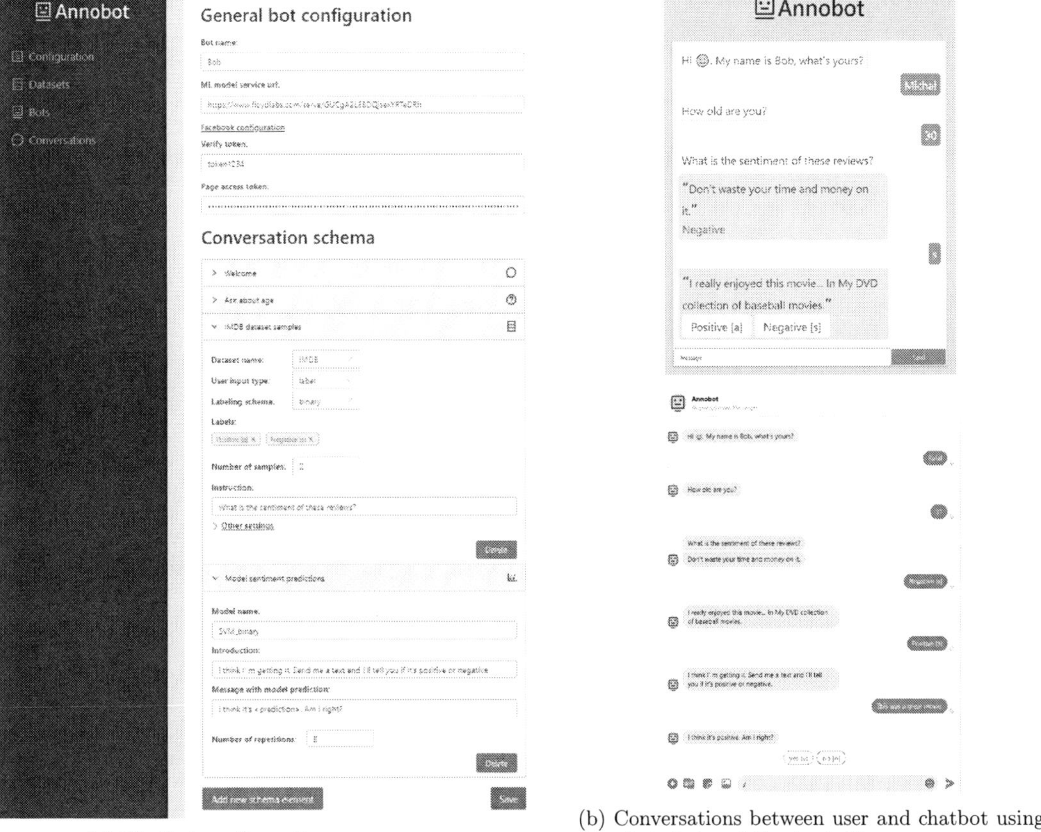

(a) Chatbot configuration.

(b) Conversations between user and chatbot using Annobot chat and Facebook Messenger.

Figure 2: Configuration and conversations with chatbot.

3.1.1 Pre-annotation

Pre-annotation is a procedure of automatic annotation of the text using the existing automatic system and presenting these annotations to the human annotator. In our system, this functionality is realized, e.g. in the form of a message sent by a chatbot to a user, in which it asks about the correctness of the classified text. The user can then confirm or deny it.

3.1.2 Active Sampling

Sampling labelling data can affect the time spent on creating a valuable collection. In our platform, we use the ML models module to implement Least Confidence (Culotta and Mccallum, 2005) active learning method. Firstly, the application sends examples with labels to it (one by one or in batches), and secondly, it uses its predictions to sort the unlabeled data.

3.1.3 Online learning

Online learning consists of continuous updating and improving the existing system/model. Data can be transferred after each assigned label or in batches. Annobot can be integrated with any model that has the appropriate REST API.

3.1.4 Inter-annotator agreement

Inter-annotator agreement (IAA) is a measure of how well two (or more) annotators can make the same annotation decision. It is an important part of any labelling tool used by several people in parallel.

77

3.2 Technology

When creating our platform, we tried to choose technologies that are well established and currently actively develop. To create web modules (chat and admin panel), we used HTML, CSS and TypeScript with ReactJs library. The core module was written in Java with the use of the Spring framework. The ML model was created in Python using libraries, such as scikit-learn, Flair and Flask. While as our data source, we used PostgreSQL database.

4 Usability Experiment

To verify the efficiency of our platform, we conduct a preliminary annotation experiment. For comparison with our system, we have chosen two tools that can be used for document annotating: Label Studio (Heartex, 2019) and Doccano (Nakayama et al., 2018). We extracted 48 reviews from the IMDB dataset (Maas et al., 2011) as the corpus to be annotated. The task was to determine the sentiment (positive or negative) of the review. The job should be performed using each system first in the desktop version and then in the mobile version using a mobile device. Therefore the experiment consisted of 6 sub-tasks (3 tools x 2 versions). To each of this sub-task, we assigned eight reviews, so that they had similar text length distribution and the same class representation. The experiment was attended by 12 people (5 women and 7 men). To eliminate the "first system" effect, participants were given instructions in which the order of the systems was different. The results are shown in Figure 3. When analyzing the average results for desktop versions, we found an only small difference between our solution and Label Studio according to the t-test with 0.05 significance level. However, the same test showed a significant difference between these systems and Doccano. Analyzing the results of the mobile version, we found that the difference between Annobot and either Label Studio or Doccano is significant at the 0.05 level, according to a t-test. In the case of mobile versions, the participants, speaking about the Annobot, unanimously pointed to intuitiveness and the form of interaction they are familiar with (they usually pointed out that they are Facebook Messenger users).

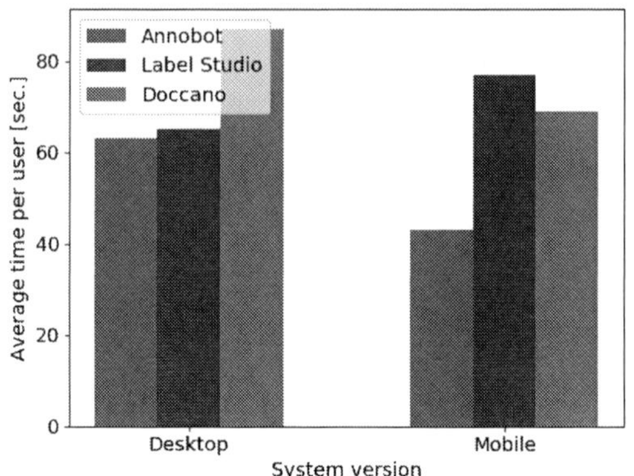

Figure 3: Average labelling time (in seconds) using Annobot, Label Studio, and Doccano in desktop and mobile versions.

5 Applications

The Annobot has many applications, such as data labelling for binary, multi-class/label classification tasks, preparing data for regression problems, or creating sets for issues such as machine translation, question answering or text summarization. If we are talking about the type of data: these can be short texts, sentences or tweets, as well as longer documents. Potential recipients of the platform may be researchers (not only in the field of computer science, but, e.g. sociologists or psychologists who can create surveys with the help of Annobot), companies that want to accelerate the development and improve their systems/models by making them accessible to the world, or ordinary people for whom teaching chatbot, e.g. to recognize what hate speech is, can be a form of participation in the development of AI, which has benefits for society.

6 Conclusion

In this paper, we propose the Annobot platform. We believe that our solution offers a lot of possibilities resulting from the form of interaction we have adopted. It is possible, for example, to introduce an element of "curiosity" of the bot, e.g., by asking about the reason for this and not another decision of the labeller. In the future, we would like to integrate our platform with Slack[4] communication platform.

References

Kalina Bontcheva, Hamish Cunningham, Ian Roberts, Angus Roberts, Valentin Tablan, Niraj Aswani, and Genevieve Gorrell. 2013. Gate teamware: a web-based, collaborative text annotation framework. *Language Resources and Evaluation*, 47(4):1007–1029, Dec.

Edward Collins, Nikolai Rozanov, and Bingbing Zhang. 2019. LIDA: Lightweight interactive dialogue annotator. In *Proceedings of the 2019 Conference on Empirical Methods in Natural Language Processing and the 9th International Joint Conference on Natural Language Processing (EMNLP-IJCNLP): System Demonstrations*, pages 121–126, Hong Kong, China, November.

Aron Culotta and Andrew Mccallum. 2005. Reducing labeling effort for structured prediction tasks. volume 2, pages 746–751, 01.

Heartex. 2019. Label Studio. Software available from https://github.com/heartexlabs/label-studio.

Jonathan K. Kummerfeld. 2019. SLATE: A super-lightweight annotation tool for experts. In *Proceedings of the 57th Annual Meeting of the Association for Computational Linguistics: System Demonstrations*, pages 7–12, Florence, Italy, July.

Bill Yuchen Lin, Dong-Ho Lee, Frank F. Xu, Ouyu Lan, and Xiang Ren. 2019. AlpacaTag: An active learning-based crowd annotation framework for sequence tagging. In *Proceedings of the 57th Annual Meeting of the Association for Computational Linguistics: System Demonstrations*, pages 58–63, Florence, Italy, July.

Andrew L. Maas, Raymond E. Daly, Peter T. Pham, Dan Huang, Andrew Y. Ng, and Christopher Potts. 2011. Learning word vectors for sentiment analysis. In *Proceedings of the 49th Annual Meeting of the Association for Computational Linguistics: Human Language Technologies*, pages 142–150, Portland, Oregon, USA, June. Association for Computational Linguistics.

Saif Mohammad, Felipe Bravo-Marquez, Mohammad Salameh, and Svetlana Kiritchenko. 2018. SemEval-2018 task 1: Affect in tweets. In *Proceedings of The 12th International Workshop on Semantic Evaluation*, pages 1–17, New Orleans, Louisiana, June.

Hiroki Nakayama, Takahiro Kubo, Junya Kamura, Yasufumi Taniguchi, and Xu Liang. 2018. doccano: Text annotation tool for human. Software available from https://github.com/doccano/doccano.

Pontus Stenetorp, Sampo Pyysalo, Goran Topić, Tomoko Ohta, Sophia Ananiadou, and Jun'ichi Tsujii. 2012. brat: a web-based tool for NLP-assisted text annotation. In *Proceedings of the Demonstrations at the 13th Conference of the European Chapter of the Association for Computational Linguistics*, pages 102–107, Avignon, France, April.

Jie Yang, Yue Zhang, Linwei Li, and Xingxuan Li. 2018. YEDDA: A lightweight collaborative text span annotation tool. In *Proceedings of ACL 2018, System Demonstrations*, pages 31–36, Melbourne, Australia, July.

Seid Muhie Yimam, Iryna Gurevych, Richard Eckart de Castilho, and Chris Biemann. 2013. WebAnno: A flexible, web-based and visually supported system for distributed annotations. In *Proceedings of the 51st Annual Meeting of the Association for Computational Linguistics: System Demonstrations*, pages 1–6, Sofia, Bulgaria, August.

Marcos Zampieri, Shervin Malmasi, Preslav Nakov, Sara Rosenthal, Noura Farra, and Ritesh Kumar. 2019. Semeval-2019 task 6: Identifying and categorizing offensive language in social media (offenseval). In *SemEval@NAACL-HLT*.

---

[4]https://slack.com/

Arabic Curriculum Analysis

Hamdy Mubarak*, Shimaa Shoukry, Ahmed Abdelali* and Kareem Darwish***
Qatar Computing Research Institute
Hamad Bin Khalifa University
Doha, Qatar
*{hmubarak,aabdelali,kdarwish}@hbku.edu.qa
Qatar University
Doha, Qatar
**st1103366@student.qu.edu.qa

Abstract

Developing a platform that analyzes the content of curricula can help identify their shortcomings and whether they are tailored to specific desired outcomes. In this paper, we present a system to analyze Arabic curricula and provide insights into their content. It allows users to explore word presence, surface-forms used, as well as contrasting statistics between different countries from which the curricula were selected. Also, it provides a facility to grade text in reference to given grade-level and gives users feedback about the complexity or difficulty of words used in a text.

1 Introduction

Effective language curricula are critical to teaching communication skills that are required in professional and academic settings. Building suitable curricula or updating existing ones is typically a laborious and time consuming process often requiring many specialists working together. Due to its complexity, it is imperative to have tools that ascertain if the curricula achieve the desired learning objectives, as measured for example by vocabulary level. Developing a platform that analyzes curricula can help identify shortcomings and whether they are tailored to desired outcomes. Natural Language Processing (NLP) can provide automated methods to perform such analysis and provide feedback to curricula developers.

A wealth of research devoted to build, curate, and assess educational materials has been published for English and other Latin languages (Tyler, 1950; Oliva, 2005; Braun et al., 2006; Soto, 2015). Though some recent NLP work on Arabic has addressed language learning, readability and textbook assessments (Zaghouani et al., 2014; Zalmout et al., 2016; Al Khalil et al., 2018), the work is limited with rather scarce resources and tools. This paper aims to contribute to curricula assessment, and fill some of the gaps in the literature. We focus on analyzing Arabic curricula taught in Gulf countries at elementary school level. We built a tool that analyzes curricula by providing: statistics about word usage and morphological forms in different grades; words belonging to specific categories, such as food or animals; comparison with other curricula; and complexity levels of words in a text according to selected grades. The tool provides insights into the strengths and weaknesses of curricula and highlights what they cover in terms of vocabulary and morphological constructs. Further, we added some features of potential help to instructors and learners. These include word pronunciation, using text-to-speech, English translation, using machine translation, diacritized forms of words, using automatic diacritization, and linguistic information, such as word segmentation and part-of-speech tagging. As far as we know, this is the first system that: i) allows for browsing and comparing word usages in Arabic curricula from different countries, and ii) showcases whether students in a particular grade would likely understand pieces of text.

2 Related Work

While the research in readability is not novel; advances in technology have permitted researchers to explore further the topic and propose formulations to approximate the difficulty of texts for readers. Benjamin et. al, (2012) surveyed the developments in the field of readability from the perspective of education, linguistics, cognitive science, and psychology, and provided recommendations for the use of

---

Proceedings of the 27th International Conference on Computational Linguistics, pages 80–86
Barcelona, Spain (Online), December 12, 2020.

such evaluation techniques. Collins-Thompson (2014) explored the challenges for automatic assessment of text readability and highlighted the opportunities for using automatic modeling to predict the reading difficulty of texts. Al-Khalifa and Al-Ajlan (2010) proposed a tool for readability analysis and applied this to curricula in Saudi Arabia. Zalmout et al. (2016) described a process to analyze the textbooks of two different English teaching methods for English as a Second Language (ESL) by using readability scoring technique. Al Khalil et al. (2018) presented an Arabic reading corpus that was collected from textbooks from first to twelfth grade from United Arab Emirates and works of fiction to enhance the inadequate resources that effected educational applications. García Salido et al. (2018) proposed a lexical tool for academic writing in Spanish and described the data extraction from a corpus of academic texts. This tool basically provides insight into how to use typical vocabulary for academic genre in order to build an entire text.

Arabic is a complex language with rich morphology. Stems are typically derived from a set of roots using predefined stem templates. Affixes can be attached to stems to generate words (surface forms). For example, the word وسيكتبونها ("wsyktbwnhA" – "and they will write it")[1] has two prefixes (*and* and *will*) and two suffixes (*they* and *it*). Further, Arabic is typically written without diacritics (or short vowels) which are essential to understand meaning and properly verbalizing words. This increases the complexity when analyzing Arabic texts.

3 Data Collection

We acquired the text versions of the Arabic subject primary school curricular textbooks from six Gulf countries covering grades 1 through 6 from either 2014 or 2015[2]. These countries[3] are: Bahrain (BH), Kuwait (KW), Oman (OM), Qatar (QA), Saudi Arabia (SA), and United Arab Emirates (AE). Statistics are shown in Table 1. Table 2 has example sentences from different grades and shows that the text from grade 1 is direct and simple and is comprised mainly of short declarative sentences. On the other hand, text from grade 6 is more complex, at the vocabulary and sentence structure levels, with longer sentences.

Country	Sentences (K)	Tokens (K)	Unique Lemmas (K)
QA	22	121	<u>6.4</u>
OM	<u>20</u>	<u>110</u>	6.8
KW	29	170	8.1
SA	**40**	**194**	**8.7**
AE	24	134	7.9
BH	31	166	8.1
All	166	895	10.5

Table 1: Corpus statistics for all grades per country. Highest and lowest numbers are written in bold and underlined fonts in order.

Grade	Example
1	دَخَلَ حَمَدُ غُرْفَةَ أُمِّهِ وَهِي مَرِيْضَة. شَاهَدَ في الغُرْفَةِ زُجَاجَةَ دَوَاءٍ، فَقَالَ في نَفْسِهِ: سَوْفَ أَتَنَاوَلُ هَذَا الدَوَاءَ
	Hamad entered his mother's room while she was sick. He saw a bottle of medicine in the room. He said...
6	إنَّ الإِنْسَانَ العَامِلَ يَجِدُ أَنَّ الأَعْمَالَ المُفِيدَةَ الَتِي يَقُومُ بِهَا تُسهِمُ في صُنْعِ الحَضَارَةِ الإِنْسَانِيَة في حِينِ...
	The working man finds that his useful work contributes to the making of human civilization, while ...

Table 2: Sample sentences from QA curriculum (from Grade 1 and Grade 6)

---

[1] Buckwalter transliteration and translation are provided.
[2] We thank The World Organization for Renaissance of Arabic Language (WORAL) for data collection and preparation.
[3] We use ISO 3166-1 alpha-2 for country codes.

4 System Description

System Architecture: An overview of the system functionalities is illustrated in Figure 1, and the system can be publicly accessed using the following URL: `curriculum.qcri.org`. After the acquisition of the textbooks collection, we used the publicly available Farasa Arabic NLP toolkit to process the text. This includes morphological segmentation (Abdelali et al., 2016), diacritization (Darwish et al., 2017); and lemmatization (Mubarak, 2018). These steps are crucial to enhance the analysis given the complexities of Arabic. Next, language experts classified lemmas into 50 categories (ex: Function Words, Human, Animal, Food, History, Politics, Travel, Religious Acts, etc.)
The system provides the following functions: Term Usage, Category, Statistics, Differences, and Text Grading. It also uses Text to Speech (TTS) , Machine Translation (MT), and Farasa Tools to pronounce, translate, and provide morphological analysis of lexical items respectively.

Design: To implement our tool, we used Django[4], a Python web framework for the rapid development of database-driven websites with high performance web applications. The framework supports model-view-controller (MVC) design patterns to separate the data model and business rules from the user interface. Accordingly, the system modules are separated to ensure reuse and support multiple users and sessions.

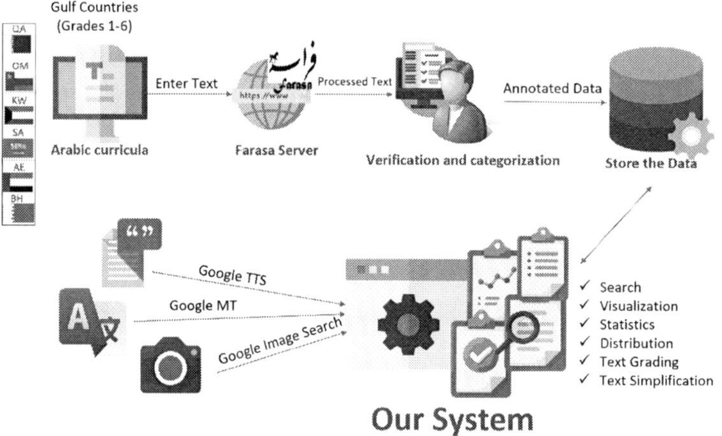

Figure 1: System architecture and functionalities

5 System Functionalities

The system provides five main functions: Term Usage, Category, Statistics, Differences, and Text Grading.

Term Usage: This provides the distribution of input words in all or a subset of grades and countries, and displays all relevant word forms as word clouds as shown in Figures 2, 3 and 4. For ambiguous words, users can select either a diacritized form or an undiacritized form. If the input word is in English, it provides the most frequent translation and displays its information. For any displayed word, users can get translation, listen to pronunciation, and obtain morphological information while hovering (Figure 3).

---

[4]`https://www.djangoproject.com/`

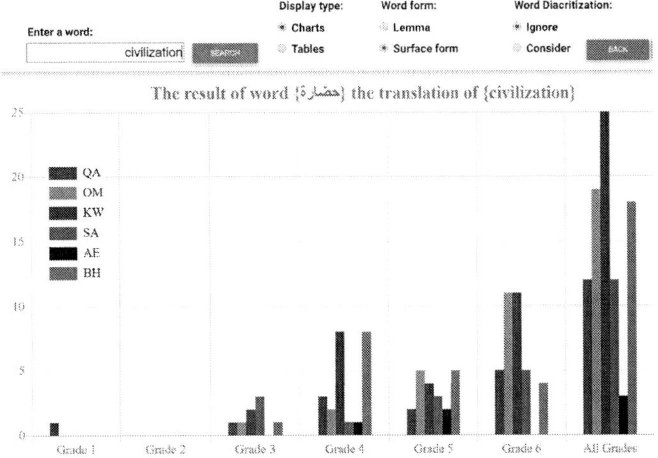

Figure 2: Frequency distributions for the word "civilization" per country and grade

Figure 3: Frequency of word forms for the lemma كتاب (ktAb) "book", translation and segmentation

Figure 4: Word cloud for surface forms of the lemma استطاع (AstTAE) "he could" in each grade

Category: Users can browse words belonging to a specific category per country and/or grade as shown in Figure 5. Such functionality gives a glimpse into the overall coverage of a given topic/category.

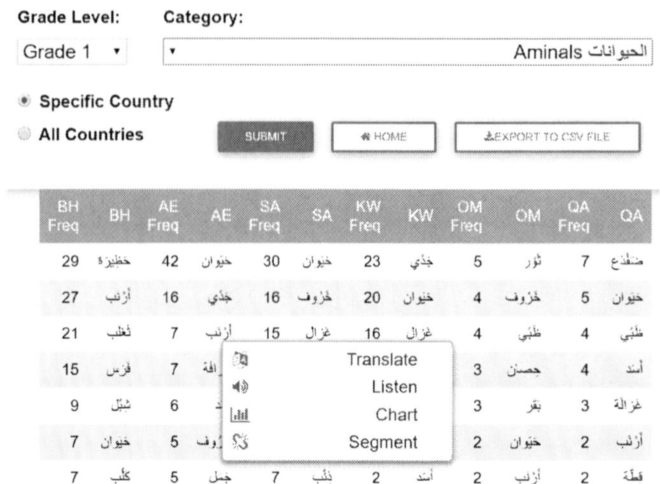

Figure 5: Listing for the "Animal" category in grade 1 per country

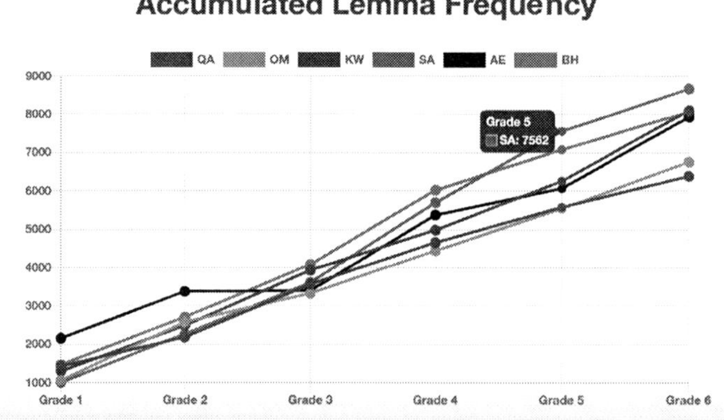

Figure 6: Accumulated lemma frequencies at each grade and for all countries

Statistics: This option shows the distribution of all the lemmas of each country and grade. Results can be shown per grade or accumulated, meaning that for each grade, results of all previous grades are also included. From Figure 6[5] we see that Arab students learn $\sim$ 1.5k lemmas in grade 1 and end up learning 8k lemmas in grade 6. Also, the curricula of QA and OM have lower vocabulary richness compared to the rest of the Gulf countries. This is very important to experts in the field of curriculum development.

Differences: To compare a curriculum of a specific country with that of other countries, users can browse words that are unique to this country in a selected grade as shown in Figure 7.

---

[5]AE files for grades 3 and 5 are incomplete, and we will solve this in the next release.

Figure 7: Words that appear uniquely in QA grade 3

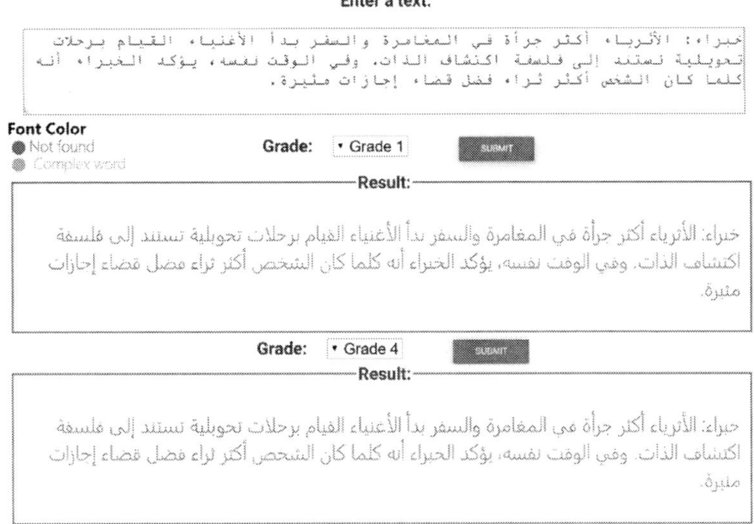

Figure 8: Text grading results for grades 1 and 4

Text Grading: This feature allows users to spot "difficult" words in a given input texts. Difficulty of a text can be measured using different methods. The system shows only words whose lemmas did not appear in the selected or preceding grades. As shown in Figure 8, for the input text, the system highlights difficult words in grade 1 (ex: خبراء، جرأة، فلسفة ("xbrA', jr>p, flsfp" – experts, audacity, philosophy)) as they are not seen in the textbooks of the selected grade. When we select higher grades, difficult words decrease. For the second example in Figure 8, the former words in the text are no longer considered difficult for grade 4 except the words تحويلية، ثراء ("tHwylyp, vrA' " – transformative, richness).

6 Conclusion and Future Work

We presented a tool for curricula analysis. For demonstration, we used a collection of elementary school grades (grades 1 to 6) from all Gulf countries. The system provides valuable insights into word usages, vocabulary coverage, and the richness of the curriculum for each grade level. Also, it provides a function for text grading in reference to a grade level, word pronunciation and translation, and morphological analysis. In the future, we aim to extend the collection to other countries and to improve text grading by considering syntactic and semantic features and give grade-level scores for input texts. We are also considering text simplification.

References

Ahmed Abdelali, Kareem Darwish, Nadir Durrani, and Hamdy Mubarak. 2016. Farasa: A fast and furious segmenter for arabic. In *Proceedings of the 2016 conference of the North American chapter of the association for computational linguistics: Demonstrations*, pages 11–16.

Hend S Al-Khalifa and Amani A Al-Ajlan. 2010. Automatic readability measurements of the arabic text: An exploratory study. *Arabian Journal for Science and Engineering*, 35(2 C):103–124.

Muhamed Al Khalil, Hind Saddiki, Nizar Habash, and Latifa Alfalasi. 2018. A leveled reading corpus of modern standard arabic. In *Proceedings of the Eleventh International Conference on Language Resources and Evaluation (LREC 2018)*, Miyazaki, Japan, May. European Language Resources Association (ELRA).

Rebekah George Benjamin. 2012. Reconstructing readability: Recent developments and recommendations in the analysis of text difficulty. *Educational Psychology Review*, 24(1):63–88.

Sabine Braun, Kurt Kohn, and J Mukherjee. 2006. *Corpus Technology and Language Pedagogy: New Resources, New Tools, New Methods. English Corpus Linguistics Vol 3.* Lang.

Kevyn Collins-Thompson. 2014. Computational assessment of text readability: A survey of current and future research. *ITL - International Journal of Applied Linguistics*, 165(2):97–135.

Kareem Darwish, Hamdy Mubarak, and Ahmed Abdelali. 2017. Arabic diacritization: Stats, rules, and hacks. In *Proceedings of the Third Arabic Natural Language Processing Workshop*, pages 9–17, Valencia, Spain, April. Association for Computational Linguistics.

Marcos García Salido, Marcos Garcia, Milka Villayandre-Llamazares, and Margarita Alonso-Ramos. 2018. A lexical tool for academic writing in spanish based on expert and novice corpora. In *Proceedings of the Eleventh International Conference on Language Resources and Evaluation (LREC 2018)*, Osaka, Japan, May. European Language Resources Association (ELRA).

Hamdy Mubarak. 2018. Build fast and accurate lemmatization for Arabic. In *Proceedings of the Eleventh International Conference on Language Resources and Evaluation (LREC 2018)*, Miyazaki, Japan, May. European Language Resources Association (ELRA).

Peter F Oliva, 2005. *Developing the curriculum (6th ed.).* Pearson, Boston.

Sandy Soto. 2015. An analysis of curriculum development. *Theory and Practice in Language Studies*, 5:1129, 06.

R. W. Tyler. 1950. *Basic Principles of Curriculum and Instruction.* University of Chicago Press.

Wajdi Zaghouani, Behrang Mohit, Nizar Habash, Ossama Obeid, Nadi Tomeh, Alla Rozovskaya, Noura Farra, Sarah Alkuhlani, and Kemal Oflazer. 2014. Large scale arabic error annotation: Guidelines and framework. In *Proceedings of the Ninth International Conference on Language Resources and Evaluation (LREC'14)*, Reykjavik, Iceland, may. European Language Resources Association (ELRA).

Nasser Zalmout, Hind Saddiki, and Nizar Habash. 2016. Analysis of foreign language teaching methods: An automatic readability approach. In *Proceedings of the 3rd Workshop on Natural Language Processing Techniques for Educational Applications (NLPTEA2016)*, pages 122–130, Osaka, Japan, December. The COLING 2016 Organizing Committee.

Epistolary Education in 21st Century: A System to Support Composition of E-mails by Students to Superiors in Japanese

Kenji Ryu

Kitami Institute of Technology
165 Koencho, Kitami,
090-8507, Japan
`m2052400085@std.kitami-it.ac.jp`

Michal Ptaszynski
Kitami Institute of Technology
165 Koencho, Kitami,
090-8507, Japan
`ptaszynski@cs.kitami-it.ac.jp`

Fumito Masui
Kitami Institute of Technology
165 Koencho, Kitami,
090-8507, Japan
`f-masui@cs.kitami-it.ac.jp`

Abstract

E-mail is a communication tool widely used by people of all ages on the Internet today, often in business and formal situations, especially in Japan. Moreover, Japanese E-mail communication has a set of specific rules taught using specialized guidebooks. E-mail literacy education for many Japanese students is typically provided in a traditional, yet inefficient lecture-based way. We propose a system to support Japanese students in writing E-mails to superiors (teachers, job hunting representatives, etc.). We firstly make an investigation into the importance of formal E-mails in Japan, and what is needed to successfully write a formal E-mail. Next, we develop the system with accordance to those rules. Finally, we evaluated the system twofold. The results, although performed on a small number of samples, were generally positive, and clearly indicated additional ways to improve the system.

1 Introduction

The development of modern means of Internet communication, such as Social Networking Services (SNS), like Facebook (https://www.facebook.com/), applications for direct chatting, like Messenger (https://www.messenger.com/), exchange of short messages, like Twitter (https://twitter.com/), images and videos, like Instagram (https://www.instagram.com/), or TikTok (https://www.tiktok.com/), fave not diminished the importance of text-based communication, as most of communication on the Internet today is still text-based. Moreover, each of such applications creates unique differences in the language use (Lin and Qiu, 2013; Jaidka et al., 2018). However, the general trend in language use across all such platforms is the colloquialisation of language, or using the language in an informal manner.

Differently to the above, the electronic mail, or E-mail has become a communication tool used by people of all ages recently mostly as a formal means of communication (Chen, 2006). Moreover, in the context of Japanese society, the E-mail, especially when used in formal situations, has a specific set of rules, manners and style, to the extent that specialized guidebooks are required to learn those[1][2]. However, for many Japanese students it is difficult to learn an effective way of writing E-mails without a proper language education, which might result in the person not finding a job after graduating the university.

Typically, E-mail writing education would include lectures where the participants study under the guidance of a teacher. However, this traditional method is inefficient as one lecture is too short to provide support to individual learners, and the cost of finding an appropriate instructor

---

[1] https://www.wasabi-jpn.com/japanese-lessons/how-to-write-emails-in-japanese-with-practical-examples/
[2] https://business-mail.jp/mail-writing

Proceedings of the 27th International Conference on Computational Linguistics, pages 87–92
Barcelona, Spain (Online), December 12, 2020.

is high. Therefore, to support Japanese students in E-mail literacy self-education, in this study, we propose a novel system for the support of writing Japanese E-mails by students to superiors.

The paper is organized as follows. We firstly describe the importance of formal E-mails in Japan, and what are the core rules and elements of a successfully written formal E-mail. Next, we describe the system and its implementation with accordance to those core rules. Furthermore, we provide the results of initial experiments aiming to evaluate the level of E-mail writing skills among Japanese students. Last section concludes the paper and sets paths for further improvement of the system and its implementation in practice in the educational system.

The system is available at m2052400085@std.kitami-it.ac.jp . When testing, send an email with "Test for E-mail composition support system" in the subject line of the E-mail.

2 Importance of Learning E-mail Literacy in Japan

2.1 Rules of Japanese E-mail Etiquette

E-mail is often used as a means of official communication between companies. Japanese university students, begin using E-mails frequently when they start looking for a job. They also use E-mails in communication with professors. In these cases, the E-mail is required to have a specific structure. It should consist of six parts, such as, "Addressee's Name", "Self-Introduction", "Preamble", "Main Body", "Closing Remarks", and "Signature". **"Addressee's Name"** should appear at the top of the E-mail, and include the name, affiliation, or an official position of the addressee. The E-mail has the address information itself, but "Addressee's Name" is needed for the addressee to know if the E-mail is addressed to them in case of the E-mail being sent to multiple people. This element is crucial when sending the message to someone who does not know the sender, but is required even if both sides know each other. **"Self-Introduction"** is necessary to appear after the "Addressee's Name", and include sender's name, affiliation, or an official position. Like "Addressee's Name", although E-mail header contains this information, "Self-Introduction" should appear in the E-mail text anyway. It can be shortened when both sides know each other, but in official situation lack of this part will result in miscommunication, or even disregarding the whole E-mail by the receiver. **"Preamble"** is an element of simple greetings. Before starting with the main text, it is necessary to include this element in the E-mail text. One should avoid simple daytime-based or seasonal greetings (e.g., こんばんは *Konbanwa* "Good evening,"), and instead use formal greeting phrases, such as いつもお世話に なります *Itsumo osewa ni narimasu* "I am in your debt for your constant help". **"Main Body"** is the main part of E-mail text. This element describes what the sender wants to discuss.There are no specific honorific phrases to use here, but introduction to the main topic should always be explicit, e.g., X の件について *X-no ken ni tsuite* "Regarding the case of X...", etc. **"Closing Remarks"** should contain simple greetings after the explanation of the topic in "Main Body". This element mainly uses text that requests the mail receiver to review the topic of the email or requests a response from the mail receiver. **"Signature"** is a detailed description of the sender's information, containing affiliation, postal code, address, E-mail address, phone number and URL for website, etc.

2.2 Education Deficiency in E-mail Literacy

Despite the importance of E-mail literacy in Japan, there has been a growing problem of deficiency in its education. For example, (Yan, 2018) studied the structure of E-mail from students to teachers focusing on comparison between Japanese native speakers and Japanese language learners (foreign students, etc.). They conducted a survey on university students asked about their learning experience of E-mail literacy. As a result,13 out of 20 (65%) Japanese students answered they never learned E-mail literacy. In January 2020, we conducted a similar survey for

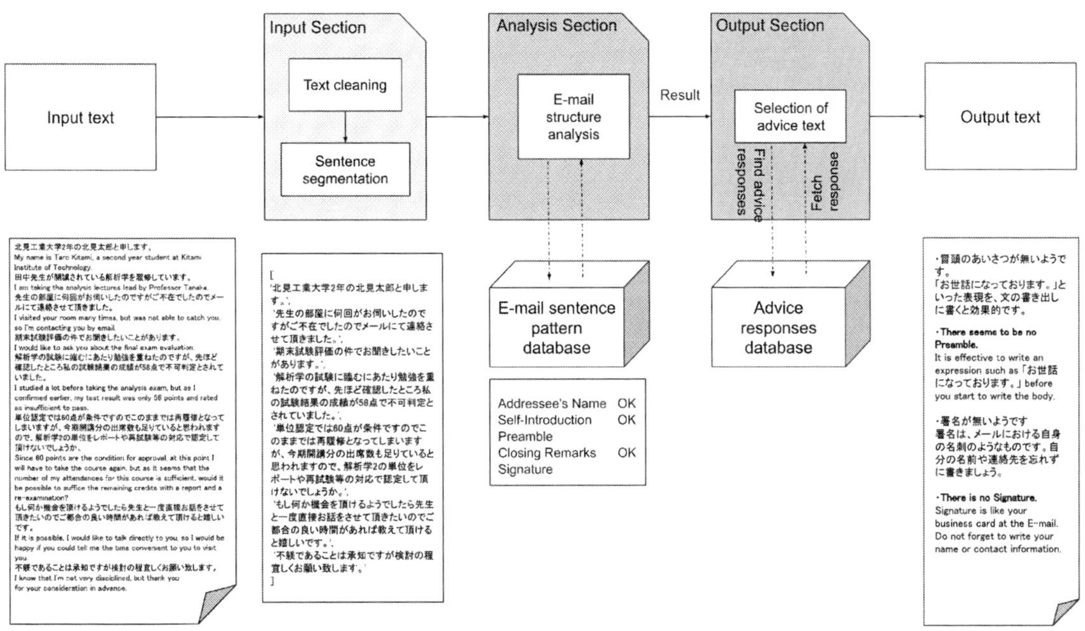

Figure 1: System overview.

students of Kitami Institute of Technology. As a result, 16 out of 23 (70%) students answered they never learned E-mail literacy. Although the sample was not large it is noticeable, that many Japanese students never learn about how to write E-mails, suggesting they do not know the rules of Japanese E-mail etiquette. This motivated us to help them and provide a system providing support and advice in writing E-mails to superiors.

3 E-mail Composition Support System

3.1 System Overview

We developed a system for E-mail structure analysis and providing a support in the form of advises about the composition of the E-mail, with an initial end-user group being university students in Japan. After analysing the contents of the email the system outputs the advice text according to the set of rules of Japanese E-mail etiquette. In the assumption the system is meant to be used as an educational tool to help Japanese students increase their E-mail literacy. The system can be separated into three main sections, namely, "Input Section", "E-mail Contents Analysis Section", "Output Section". **"Input Section"** is responsible for obtaining the text of the E-mail, and performing initial preprocessing such as text cleaning (removing unnecessary spaces, and symbols) or sentence segmentation for further analysis. **"Analysis Section"** is responsible for a structure analysis based on specific E-mail patterns. These patterns were created from the annotated data of Japanese E-mail examples collected in advance. **"Output Section"** is responsible for providing specific advises depending on the result of analysis from the previous section. Moreover, this section provides explanations about how to successfully compose E-mails in Japanese, with particular focus on the missing elements. These advises were created based on the guidelines collected from a number of guidebooks for Japanese E-mail etiquette (Fujita, 2013; Setsuko Murano, 2014; Iwamoto, 2016; Matsuoka, 2017; Tojo, 2010; Mizue, 2017; Hirano, 2017).

3.2 Data Collection and Annotation

In order to analyse E-mail text, we collected 116 example E-mail sentences from part of previously mentioned guidebooks and annotated the elements of each E-mail. Annotation task was

Addressor's Name	田中教授 Professor Tnaka,
Preamble	お世話になっております。 Hello sir, I hope all is fine.
Self-Introduction	北見大学　デザイン工学科3年　北見太郎と申します。 My name is Taro Kitami and I'm a 3rd year student in the Department of Design Engineering at Kitami University.
Main Body	今回は、解析学Ⅰのレポート提出の件で、ご連絡いたしました。 I'm contacting you about submitting a report for Analysis 1 class this time. 解析学Ⅰのレポートを添付させていただきます。 The report for Analysis I is attached.
Closing Remarks	お忙しいところ恐縮ですが、ご確認のほどお願いいたします。 I'm terribly sorry to disturb you, but I would appreciate it for your confirmation.
Signature	北見大学　デザイン工学科 3年　北見太郎 mail　test@std.kitami-it.ac.jp 〒 090-8507 国立大学法人　北見大学 北海道北見市田舎町1番地

Figure 2: Annotated sentence

done by 7 annotators, who annotated sentences of the examples with classes representing each necessary element of the E-mail. Using the data from each elements, we manually extracted patterns that best represent each E-mail element, to use them in the analysis.

3.3 System Implementation

The main part of the E-mail Composition Support System was written in Python3. The input text for the analysis was obtained via custom Mail server, as is the output with the advises provided to the users. As for the mail server, we used "Postfix" (http://www.postfix.org/) as the SMTP Server, and "Dovecot" (https://www.dovecot.org/) as the POP/IMAP Server. Combining these software, the system can receive E-mails from the users and send the results of analysis to the users automatically.

4 Evaluation Experiments

4.1 Validation on Development Dataset

To evaluate our system, we performed two experiments. Firstly, we tested the system on data containing 20 Japanese E-mail examples collected from Japanese E-mail etiquette guidebooks, that were not included in initial training data.

As a result of this experiment, in 17 out of 20 cases (85%) the system was able to detect all the elements and provide output confirming that the E-mail contains all the necessary elements. When it comes to the error cases, the reason for the three cases where the system generated incorrect output, was that the E-mails contained sentence patterns that were not originally included in the system, thus the system could not detect some elements correctly.

We improved the analysis performance by adding the new patterns the system could not analyse correctly in the first experiment.

Input text	Correct cases	Incorrect cases	Total
example sentences	17	3	20
written by students	6	0	6

Table 1: Results of experiments.

4.2 User-based Evaluation

In the second experiment, we tested the system on E-mails written by six Japanese students to test the performance of E-mail structure analysis in practice. As a result of the second experiment with improved system, in all cases the system detected the presence or absence of the elements, and provide output that adapt the result of analysis. All of those cases represented specifically prepared scenarios where the students were to ask their supervising professors for help. Although the results were positive, we acknowledge that we need more subjects set in various scenarios to have a more objective evaluation of the system.

5 Conclusion and Future Work

In this paper, we described an E-mail Composition Support System aimed to be used as an educational tool for Japanese students to increase their E-mail literacy. The development of this system was stemmed by two factors, namely, (1) the importance for the young people in Japan to master E-mail literacy, and (2) the deficiency in its education in reality. The twofold evaluation of the system showed positive results, and clearly indicated ways to further improve the system. In the near future we plan to implement this system in the educational curriculum for the classes on Communication Literacy, which will also allow additional robust evaluation on at least five hundred students.

References

Chi-Fen Emily Chen. 2006. The development of e-mail literacy: From writing to peers to writing to authority figures. *Language Learning & Technology*, 10(2):35–55.

Eiji Fujita. 2013. メール文章力の基本大切だけど、だれも教えてくれない 77のルール *"77 Rules That Nobody Tell You - The Basics of E-mail writing"*. 日本実業出版社 Nippon Jitsugyo Publishing.

Tomoaki Hirano. 2017. イラッとされないビジネスメール　正解　不正解 *"Business Emails that Won't Anyone Irritate - Correct and Incorrect Answers"*. サンクチュアリ出版 Sanctuary Publishing.

Akinori Iwamoto. 2016. メールの書き方（基礎編）*"how to write e-mail(basics)"*. http://www2.ipcku.kansai-u.ac.jp/~iwamoto/howtowriteanemail0.pdf, April.

Kokil Jaidka, Sharath Chandra Guntuku, and Lyle H Ungar. 2018. Facebook versus twitter: Differences in self-disclosure and trait prediction. In *Twelfth International AAAI Conference on Web and Social Media*.

Han Lin and Lin Qiu. 2013. Two sites, two voices: Linguistic differences between facebook status updates and tweets. In *International Conference on Cross-Cultural Design*, pages 432–440. Springer.

Kazumi Matsuoka. 2017. メールを書くときにはここに注意 *"tips you should care for writing e-mail"*. http://user.keio.ac.jp/ matsuoka/mailsample.htm, September.

Hiroyoshi Mizue. 2017. そのまま使える! ビジネスメール文例辞典 *"Business Email Dictionary - You can use it right away!"*. 株式会社秀和システム Shuwa System Co.,LTD.

Mariko Yamabe Setsuko Murano, Yoko Mukoyama. 2014. 上級レベル　タスクで学ぶ日本語ビジネスメール・ビジネス文書 *"Advance Level - Learning Japanese Business E-mail and Documents with Tasks"*. スリーエーネットワーク 3ANetwork.

Fumichiyo Tojo. 2010. すぐに役立つビジネス文書 & メール文例事典 *"Dictionary of Useful Business Documents & E-mail Examples"*. 池田書店 Ikeda Publishing CO.,LTD., March.

Wei Yan. 2018. Consideration on form and expression of mail from students to teachers : focusing on comparison between japanese native speaker and learner. 日本語研究 *Nihongo kenkyuu (Japanse Language Research)*, (38):17–31, Jun.